THAT MEN SHALL BE FREE

The Story of the Magna Carta

All Americans cherish the privileges of liberty
granted to them by the Bill of Rights. These
principles of freedom were conceived in a remark-
able document called the Magna Carta. Over five
centuries before the American Revolution, a few
Englishmen dared to wrest these rights from
kings who considered themselves above all laws.
King John and his predecessors, by continual ex-
tortion of money and violations of feudal customs,
aroused the wrath of the barons who, though they
lived in comparative luxury, objected to being
subject to the king's whims. When John openly
opposed the Church, the noblemen revolted. At
the center of this conflict stood one of the unsung
heroes of history, Stephen Langton, Archbishop
of Canterbury. He helped the noblemen draft the
Magna Carta, which granted men rights that were
later considered inalienable. How these rights
were threatened and how men have battled and
died for them through history, is a part of the
story that has never ended.

Books by Clifford Lindsey Alderman

JOSEPH BRANT
Chief of the Six Nations

THAT MEN SHALL BE FREE
The Story of the Magna Carta

THAT MEN SHALL BE FREE

The Story of the Magna Carta

by

Clifford Lindsey Alderman

Drawings by Barry Martin

JULIAN MESSNER, INC.
NEW YORK

Published by Julian Messner, Inc.
8 West 40th Street, New York 10018

© Copyright 1964 by Clifford Lindsey Alderman

THAT MEN SHALL BE FREE

The Story of the Magna Carta

13th Century Britain

1

On a sunny morning in April, 1760, with a spanking breeze churning up whitecaps that capered merrily in the blue harbor, the brigantine *Sarah* lay moored at a wharf on the Boston waterfront. All seemed quiet aboard, almost as though the ship had gone to sleep, tired after the voyage from which she had arrived early that morning. As she felt the surge of the incoming flood tide, she stirred a little, her mooring lines creaked drowsily, and the tops of her two masts, which seemed nearly to touch the sky in their graceful upward sweep, swayed slightly.

Suddenly the quiet was broken by the tramp of feet along the wharf, and a shout: "Aboard the *Sarah,* there! Where's the captain?"

A man dressed in a tarred canvas jacket, wide-flared breeches and a broad-brimmed, varnished hat leaned over the bulwarks. "Who wants him?" he asked.

"We're customs officers," said one of the five men.

7

"I'm the mate," said the man on deck. "What's this all about?"

"Tell the captain we want to see your manifest."

"Come aboard," said the mate. He turned and disappeared down a deck hatchway. A few moments later he returned with the brigantine's master.

"Here you are," said the captain, handing the leader of the customs men the ship's manifest. "All in order, you see. Our cargo's indigo and logwood, loaded in the British Antilles."

The official scanned the manifest briefly. "Open up your hatches," he demanded. "We'll have a look at your cargo."

The shipmaster frowned. "You'd better see John Erving, the owner, about that. I've got no orders to open the hatches."

"Never mind him. We've got authority to search your ship."

"I can't do anything without Mr. Erving's orders," the captain answered.

The customs officer nodded to his four companions. "Get the hatch covers off."

The captain beckoned to the mate. "Go ashore as fast as you can, Jenkins, and fetch Mr. Erving from his countinghouse. Tell him there's trouble aboard."

The mate had scarcely galloped off the wharf before the customs men, armed with mallets, had knocked out the battens and removed the cover of the main deck cargo hatch. The leader peered into the hold. "Logwood and indigo, eh?" he growled. "First time I've ever seen 'em in hogsheads."

Turning to one of his men he said, "Jump down into the hold and start the bung from one of those hogsheads."

The man knocked out a bung, dipped his finger into the bunghole, licked it and grinned up at his superior. "Molasses," he said.

"Just as we thought," replied the official. He drew a paper from his waistcoat pocket. "Put this plaster on her," he told another of his assistants.

By the time the man had nailed the paper to the mainmast, the mate had returned from the countinghouse, which was just off the wharf. Puffing along beside him was a portly, dignified gentleman in coat and knee breeches of blue broadcloth, an embroidered, canary-yellow waistcoat and silver-laced cocked hat. Red-faced with exertion, John Erving, one of the richest merchant shipowners in the great town of Boston, strode up to the customs official.

"What does this mean?" he demanded.

The official pointed to the notice on the mainmast. "Your ship has been seized and libeled for smuggling molasses, sir, loaded in the French Antilles in violation of His Majesty's Navigation Acts."

"How dare you open that hatch without permission!" Erving raged.

The official drew out a second document and handed it to the merchant. "There's our authority, sir—a writ of assistance issued by the Superior Court in the name of His Majesty, George III. It allows us to search your vessel or any other place for smuggled cargo."

News of what was going on aboard the *Sarah* had spread quickly along the waterfront. Several other merchants had already come aboard, and others were streaming down the wharf. They gathered in an angry knot about the customs official.

"It's an outrage!" one declared. "Why shouldn't we trade

with the French Antilles? Provisions fetch a good price there. So does a return cargo of molasses here."

"You're allowed to bring in molasses, sir," said the customs man, "but you've got to declare it, as you know very well."

"Aye," snorted the merchant, "and pay the ruinous duty on it. A man has a right to make a living."

"What about Rhode Island?" another merchant demanded. "The customs men don't go snooping around there. Those fellows'd give 'em a suit of tar and feathers if they tried it."

"In the Connecticut province too," said another.

The official shrugged. "As to that I can't say. My orders came from Mr. Paxton."

"Paxton!" a voice cried. "We've had naught but trouble since Charles Paxton became surveyor of the port. Him and his writs of assistance! Why, a man has no rights of privacy at all. You and your men will go poking into our ships and our warehouses, and even our homes, for all I know."

"And what about Paxton's spies?" said another. "How do you suppose he knew the *Sarah* had molasses? One of his paid informers in John Erving's countinghouse, I'll warrant you. He's got them planted everywhere."

"Gentlemen, gentlemen!" John Erving interposed, "we'll get nowhere with talk." He inclined his head toward the customs official. "This officer is only doing his duty. Jemmy Otis is our man. We'll get him to bring the matter of the writs of assistance to court."

A chorus of approval went up from the others. "Aye," said one, "Jemmy's a sharp lawyer. He'll have us our rights."

All were agreed that the suggestion was a good one. With other Boston merchants they banded together and asked James Otis if he would represent them as their counsel and bring a suit charging that the writs of assistance were illegal. Later, in the days when the American Revolution was brewing, Otis would become one of the greatest and most devoted American patriots. Already he was convinced that the colonists' rights were being taken away by England.

"As advocate general of the Court of Admiralty, I am a lawyer for the Crown," he explained, "so I am unable to take a case against it. But this is an important matter. Your liberties as British subjects are being violated. I will resign my appointment and represent you."

"How much will you charge us?" they wanted to know.

"Nothing," Otis replied. "In such a case I despise all fees!"

Meanwhile, the case against the *Sarah*'s owner for smuggling molasses came up before the Court of Admiralty, which ruled in suits concerned with shipping. John Erving was found guilty and sentenced to pay a fine of half the value of his ship and her cargo.

No one could deny that the decision was a just one. Under British law, trading with countries other than England, or their colonies, was forbidden, though molasses could be brought in if the high customs duty was paid. Most New England merchants did engage in such trade whenever they could make a good profit, especially in sugar and molasses from the French islands of the West Indies. The laws against it were unpopular and had long been disregarded. Now the British government was trying to stop smuggling by issuing writs of assistance allowing the customs men to search where they pleased for contraband.

The suit against the writs of assistance was a very different matter. Otis was determined to bring it before the Superior Court of the Massachusetts Bay Colony and to prove that the writs violated the rights of American colonists as Englishmen. It took him a long time, but at last in February, 1761, the trial was held in the Town House of Boston.

The great square Council Chamber was dim that day in the wintry gray light that came through its windows, but the fire blazing on the hearth of its cavernous fireplace shed a flickering illumination upon an imposing assemblage. A young lawyer, seated at the long table reserved for barristers-at-law, looked curiously about him. He was a round, plump little man with a ruddy complexion, light brown hair and a pair of blue eyes that glistened with excitement and missed nothing of the scene about him. As the trial proceeded, this man, John Adams, who would one day become a great President of the United States, wrote a description of all that he saw and heard on that eventful day in American history.

He was not supposed to be there at all. A man had to practice law for three years before he could be admitted as a barrister, and John had not been at it that long. He was delighted that he and another young lawyer, Josiah Quincy, who sat beside him, had been able to persuade the court to let them attend.

The others at the table were older men, dignified in their long black robes and tiewigs, eager to hear the pleading in this case which affected the liberties of all American colonists. Behind them, on three long rows of chairs beneath the big chandelier hung in the center of the chamber, sat the sixty-three merchants who had brought the suit, gorgeous in coats, waistcoats and knee breeches of many colors.

John Adams' eyes shifted toward the front of the Council Chamber. Most imposing of all were the five judges, ranged about the fireplace in robes of scarlet with wide white bands of cambric at the neck, and vast wigs which tumbled to their shoulders and gave them an air of indescribable authority. Alongside them were Governor Francis Bernard and his council, also resplendent in velvet and satin, their swords and gold-laced hats gleaming in the firelight from a table nearby.

Before these personages sat Jeremiah Gridley, the King's attorney who would defend the suit, and the prosecution, James Otis and Oxenbridge Thacher, who had also agreed to represent the merchants without any fee. John Adams knew all three. It was odd to see them here like this. Mr. Gridley had trained both Otis and Thacher in the law. Now the pupils were going to try and give the teacher a lesson in it.

Gazing down from their frames on the wall were two kings of England, Charles II and James II, painted full length in oil. In their robes of ermine and purple, both appeared stern, as though they resented any attempt by these upstart subjects of the Crown to question the royal authority.

Chief Justice Thomas Hutchinson, who was also lieutenant-governor of the colony, nodded to the clerk of the court, who banged his mace three times on the floor and three times shouted, "Oyez!" as he opened the court. Jeremiah Gridley got to his feet and addressed the judges.

He had a good argument. The writs of assistance were legal in England, he told the court. "If it is law in England, it is law here, extended to this country by act of Parliament."

Then mild-mannered Oxenbridge Thacher rose and began to speak. John Adams had an uneasy feeling that he was not convincing, that he was not proving what he said he would prove. But when James Otis stood before the court and plunged into his argument, John felt better.

Otis was a great hulking giant of a man with a short,

thick neck set above shoulders as broad as an ox yoke, bold, wild eyes, and a voice as big as the rest of him. When he stood silent for a moment before the court, with his head lowered, it was for all the world as though he were a raging bull poised to charge and send chairs and judges alike flying in all directions like so many bowling pins. But instead he turned and began to plow back and forth before them while he shattered the writs of assistance like so much kindling.

Such was the power of that bellowing voice that it held judges, merchants and lawyers alike spellbound. At the start of the trial, John Adams had seized one of the quill pens on the table before him and started scribbling down his impressions. Now he forgot to write and hung on every word Otis spoke. Later he wrote that Otis was a "flame of fire."

"This writ is against the fundamental principles of English law," Otis thundered. "A man's house is his castle, and while he is quiet he is as secure as a prince in his castle. Only for felonies may an officer break and enter, and then by special—not general—warrant."

John Adams saw the merchants sit up and brighten at that. The customs officers were using the writs of assistance as general warrants, allowing them to search at any time without warning. If Otis could prove they were special warrants, a new one, sworn to by an informer, would have to be issued for each search. That might give the merchants time to move smuggled cargo to a hiding place where it would not be found.

Otis talked on and on. The winter twilight began to fall, and candles were lighted in the Council Chamber. Suddenly John Adams pricked up his ears. Otis was talking about the old Saxon laws of England, and of the famous document known as Magna Carta, which gave men certain rights and liberties—he glanced up at the portraits on the wall—and which had been used against kings like the Charleses and the Jameses when they became tyrannical.

What Otis was saying now had a familiar ring: "If a man be taken or committed to prison against the law of the land, what remedy hath the party grieved? He may have an action grounded up this Great Charter. . . ."

Coke! James Otis was quoting Sir Edward Coke on Magna Carta. The famous English lawyer had lived in the sixteenth century and had studied and written learnedly about this Great Charter which King John's rebellious barons had forced him to sign in the meadow of Runnymede in the year 1215.

John Adams had learned about Magna Carta from the writings of Sir Edward Coke. As a clerk in an attorney's office while he was studying law, he had been made to read Coke's treatises and write a condensed summary of them. More than one law student had given up in despair after trying to understand what the eminent British lawyer had been driving at, but John had waded through the books. Now he could understand why James Otis was quoting Coke on Magna Carta. In this suit, known as Paxton's Case, a principle of the liberties all Englishmen enjoyed because of Magna Carta was being threatened.

James Otis did not win a victory for the merchants. Although he had made a convincing demonstration that the writs of assistance were unconstitutional, the five judges decided unanimously that they were legal. But Otis had won a far greater victory. It was not the first time that Magna Carta had been used in America, for its principles and even its language had been adopted in writing many colonial charters and laws. Using it in court to proclaim the rights of American colonists, Otis had defied the Parliament in England to take away those rights, guaranteed to English subjects under Magna Carta and English law which had been created from that great document.

John Adams never forgot what he had seen and heard. Years later, in writing his memoirs, he said, "Here this day, in the old Council Chamber, the child Independence was born."

Why is Magna Carta, written more than seven hundred years ago, important to all Americans today, just as it was then, in 1761? What were the principles it contained which made it a cornerstone of freedom, first for Englishmen and then for Americans? How did it come to be written?

The story begins long ago in the Middle Ages when the kings of England were all-powerful and often tyrants. Like every good melodrama, it has a villain and a hero. And as in every good melodrama, the villain, John, King of England, after years of wicked rule, was at last vanquished by the hero, Stephen Langton, Archbishop of Canterbury.

2

It all resulted from the power which rested in the hands of the kings of England in the Middle Ages because of the land they held. No one else really "owned" any. The king granted portions of it to his barons, who included not only those with the title of baron, but the higher-ranking earls and other noblemen. Thus they became his vassals, swearing to fight for him in war and to counsel and support him at all times.

The more powerful barons, who often held several vast estates in different parts of England, in turn had their vassals, the lesser knights, to whom they granted portions of these lands. Finally, the land was divided into small farms granted to peasants.

Some of these latter were called "freemen" because they had enough money to pay rent for the land they farmed. Others, known as villeins, were too poor to pay rent; instead they had to spend part of their time working for their noble lords and also paying them with part of what their farms produced. This was the feudal system, which prevailed for centuries.

As long as the nobles kept their oaths to support him, the king was secure. But if enough barons turned against him, his power was lost. They could force him to do whatever they wished, or even topple him from his throne.

No monarch of England had had so much power as King Henry II when he came to the throne in 1154. He ruled not only over England, Wales and Ireland, but also Normandy in France, as all English kings had done since the Normans had conquered England in 1066. When Henry married Queen Eleanor of Aquitaine, he obtained control of that large French province. Another one, Brittany, came to him upon the death of its ruler, his brother. Thus his realm across the English Channel was vast, taking in most of what is now western and southwestern France.

With such widespread domains, Henry II might have used his power to become a tyrant, but on the whole he ruled wisely and well. He overhauled the entire government of England and made it run as smoothly as a fine watch movement, which meant taking away some of the power of the barons. They resented it, but Henry was clever enough to treat them fairly and grant them favors which kept them loyal.

Henry II had his troubles, however, with all of his sons—Henry, Richard, Geoffrey and John. They were spoiled, ungovernable, selfish, with no more docility than a pack of young wolves and less loyalty than so many weasels.

John, the youngest, was born December 24, 1167. His birth on Christmas Eve did not destine him to be a holy man, however. When he grew up he became a most unholy tyrant.

At an early age, John had seen much of the immense territory his father ruled and what great power it gave him. Henry II was a restless man, driven on by an intense energy, and he and his court were forever on the move, going from one to another of his more than sixty castles, including those on his lands in France.

John began to think how fine it would be to become a powerful ruler like his father. But since he was the youngest of the four sons, his chances of ever being king were slim. However, fate soon began to work in his favor.

When he was about five years old, his mother's love for his father turned to hate, and she left for Aquitaine. She poisoned her sons' minds against their father, and together she and young Henry, Richard and Geoffrey began plotting against him. They made an alliance with the French king, Louis VII, and attacked Henry II's lands in France. When, after two years of bitter fighting, Henry put down the rebellion, his traitorous sons fell on their knees, begged their father's mercy, swore never to rebel again and were forgiven.

They did not mean a word of their promises, and soon they began quarreling among themselves over how much each was to share once they succeeded in overthrowing their father. Young Henry and Geoffrey were allied against Richard, and in the midst of the quarrel young Henry was stricken with a fever and died. Three years later Geoffrey died of a wound received while jousting at a tournament.

Now only Richard preceded John as heir to the throne of England. The youngest prince had taken no part in his brothers' treason, but he was watching his chances. He was as treacherous as the others, returned none of the love his father lavished on him, and longed to have his one remain-

ing brother out of the way. But Richard would be a danger-
ous enemy. John waited, resolving to do whatever seemed
best for his own fortunes.

Richard, allied with a new French king, Philip Augustus,
tried again to seize his father's domains in France. Henry II
fought them, but he was growing old, bowed down, too, by
grief over the deceitfulness of his sons. Only one thought
sustained him—John, youngest and best loved of them, had
not forsaken him.

At last he was forced to yield to Richard and his French
ally. He had one request to make of his conquerors—that
they furnish him with a list of those who had turned against
him. It would have been better had he not seen it, for
John's name headed the list. Sensing that his father had not
long to live, he had cast his lot with Richard. Two days
later, on July 6, 1189, Henry II died, a heartbroken man,
and Richard became king.

He reigned only ten years, but they were evil years in
which he destroyed all the good his father had accomplished.
He did not stay in England while he wreaked his mischief
upon the country, but went off to Jerusalem on a crusade.
He was a bold, fierce warrior, despite the blackness of his
character, and his exploits won him the name of Richard
the Lionhearted.

In the years of his absence the only thought he gave to
his people in England was how he could get more money
out of them. He had left the country in the hands of two
men, known as justiciars, who were supposed to govern in
his stead. Their principal task, however, was to collect the
crushing taxes Richard wrung from the nobles, the Church
and the wretched peasants who could least afford it.

The moment his brother departed, John began scheming to seize the throne. When he learned that Richard, returning from his crusade, had been captured and held in Germany for a tremendous ransom, he was jubilant. But since the barons were bound by their oaths to ransom their King, the money was raised by imposing higher taxes on the miserable peasants.

The day came, however, when Richard was destroyed by his own greed. In France, waging war on his former ally, Philip Augustus, he heard of a fabulous treasure hidden in the castle of Chalus. While he was besieging the place, an arrow struck him in the neck, the wound became infected and he died.

What had seemed impossible had happened at last. John was across the Channel in a trice, and now *he* was king.

In Rouen, where he was crowned ruler of Normandy, he showed his arrogance and contempt for those gathered to honor him by laughing and chattering all through the ceremony. Just as the Archbishop of Coutances handed him a lance bearing the banner of his title as Duke of Normandy, John turned to exchange a joke with his friends and the lance clattered to the floor. Whispers went up among the spectators: "An omen! This prince, who cannot hold onto the lance of his office, will not be able to hold onto Normandy."

It bothered John not at all. Then, on May 27, 1199, he was crowned King of England at Westminster Abbey in London. This third of the line of English kings, known as the Plantagenets, was not an imposing figure as he stood in his rich coronation robes before the assemblage of nobles and churchmen, for he was short in stature. But his haughty bearing made up for the lack. His large eyes, set beneath heavy brows in a broad face, were at once bold, suspicious and shifty. They seemed to be saying:

"We are King now. We shall do as we please. Dare to stand in our way and we will destroy you. Plot against us and we will surely find you out and take our vengeance."

He swore he would love and protect the Church of Rome, abolish all bad laws and substitute good ones, and see that true justice was done in his kingdom. These were mere promises he never intended to carry out.

Very soon his troubles began. Arthur of Brittany, the son of his dead brother Geoffrey, was regarded as the rightful king by the nobles of that region. Philip Augustus gave fifteen-year-old Arthur his support and invaded Normandy. John assembled an army, went to France, defeated his enemies, captured Arthur and imprisoned the boy in the castle of Falaise in Normandy. Not long afterward the young prince vanished. No one has ever known with certainty what happened to him, but the evidence is strong that John either murdered him with his own hands or hired someone to do it.

Philip Augustus continued the war, laying siege to a number of John's Norman castles. The English king could have hurled his army against the besiegers, but twelve-year-old Isabella of Angoulême, whom he had recently married, had so bewitched him that he could find no time for fighting. After several of his castles had fallen, he received word that the French king had captured another. "Let him," he said. "Whatever he takes, we shall regain in a day."

The time came when there remained no day in which to recapture them. He had lost them all, and with them Normandy, which had been under English rule for one hundred and thirty-eight years. The ill omen of his crowning at

Rouen had come true. It was the first weakening of his power that in time was to undo him, for he would no longer have the support of his vassals in Normandy. At the same time the power of the English barons to resist him was thus increased, though as yet they were still loyal.

Their loyalty was put to a stern test when John returned to England. He summoned those of his barons who had not gone to fight with him in Normandy.

"You have failed to keep your oaths to support us," he charged.

It was not true, for when they prepared to embark for France, John had been short of money. He had taken all that these barons had brought for their own expenses and sent them home.

"Since you failed to go with us to France," he continued, "we require you to pay a tax of one-seventh of the value of all your chattels."

The barons looked at one another in consternation. One seventh of all their movable property, such as livestock, tools, implements and furniture of their baronial manors? There were angry mutterings of resentment, but there were not enough barons affected to resist the King's power, and they paid. And for no reason at all, John also decreed that all clergy to whom he had granted land must pay the same oppressive tax.

Meanwhile, a man named Stephen Langton was living quietly in Paris. He was the last one in the world to be thought of as the chief cause of John's eventual downfall. He had never seen the King, nor had John ever seen him. As far as Langton knew, he would go on to the end of his days being a humble scholar and teacher.

No one knows exactly when Stephen Langton was born,

though it was probably about two years before John, in 1165. His parents were modest landholders in Lincolnshire, and he seemed destined to become a farmer like his father. Perhaps it was some priest in the church of Lincoln, a few miles from his home, who saw that Stephen was an unusual boy; at any rate, he was sent to school, and about the year 1180 went to France and became a student at the University of Paris.

One day after a class in theology, a handsome young man came up to him.

"You seemed to be the only one besides me who paid any attention to the lecture," he said in French with a strong foreign accent. "Are you interested in theology?"

"Very much," replied Stephen.

"So am I," said the young man. "I am Lotario de' Conti di Segni, from near Rome. Since we both enjoy the study of religion, let us be friends."

Stephen felt flattered, for he could see by Lotario's dress and manner that he must be one of the nobility, as indeed he was, the son of an Italian count.

They were friends and companions until Lotario obtained his degree of master of arts and prepared to leave Paris.

"My uncle is a cardinal at the Vatican in Rome," he told Stephen. "He has summoned me there to become a canon in the Church of St. Peter. Tell me, what do you plan to do when you have your degree?"

"I want to teach theology," Stephen said. "I hope to set up my own school here in Paris. And I want to spend a great deal of time studying the meanings of the Bible."

"Yes, you are a scholar," said Lotario, "but as a scholar you will live almost like a monk. It seems to me that one who has your talents could go farther than that."

"I shall be happy in my work."

"Nevertheless, I hope this parting will not mean we shall never see each other again. I am sure we will."

With Rome so far away, Stephen was doubtful that it would happen. He followed his own plan and started a school of theology. Feeling that the system of instruction in the subject was poor, he reorganized it. He also wrote treatises on religion and composed a famous hymn, *Veni, Sancte Spiritus*. Some historians say he was the first to divide the Bible into chapters, as it appears today.

Strangely, although Stephen Langton had no idea he would play an important part in obtaining the rights and freedoms of men, they were much in his mind. Lecturing at the Sorbonne, one of the colleges composing the university, he spoke of the relation between a king and his subjects.

"The subject owes obedience only as long as the king acts according to law, and upon the advice of his proper counselors," he said. That was to be the very heart of Magna Carta —that the King of England was not above the law.

In Rome, Stephen's old friend of the university had made fine strides. When Pope Gregory VIII died, Lotario's uncle, the cardinal, became Pope Clement III, and elevated his nephew to a cardinal. In 1198, when Clement III died, the College of Cardinals, meeting in solemn conclave, chose Lotario de' Conti di Segni as Pope, and he took the name of Innocent III.

In England, Hubert Walter, Archbishop of Canterbury, died. He had acquired immense power, not only as head of the Church in England, a country then wholly Catholic, but he had virtually ruled the kingdom as chief justiciar while Richard was away.

John, who hated and feared anyone whose power might

threaten his own, was overjoyed when he heard of Walter's death. "Now, for the first time, I am really King of England!" he exulted.

Determined that the new archbishop would do as he was told and not meddle with the affairs of government, he hastened to Canterbury.

"We demand that you elect John Grey, Bishop of Norwich, as your archbishop," he told the prior and the monks.

They were outraged that he should dictate their choice, but they knew how vindictive he was, and what terrible vengeance he might take if they disobeyed him. Obediently, they elected John Grey.

The King went back to London, well pleased with himself. Then, to his consternation, a staggering piece of news reached him. Immediately after Walter's death, some of the Canterbury monks, meeting secretly by night, had elected one of their number, a subprior named Reginald, as archbishop. Sworn to silence, Reginald had departed for Rome to be confirmed by the Pope, but on reaching Flanders had indiscreetly bragged of the great office which had come to him.

John had a frightful temper, and flew into a maniacal rage. He summoned a delegation of the Canterbury monks before him.

"We will show these vipers among you that no one disputes our authority!" he stormed. "If you value your lives, be off to Rome instantly, and take this letter we have written to the Pope, telling him that John Grey is the rightful head of the Church in England."

It was at this very time that Stephen Langton, cloistered in Paris, received an astonishing message. His companion of their college days had not forgotten his wish that the two might later be reunited. Innocent III had summoned him to Rome to become a cardinal.

He was there when the monk Reginald and the King's delegation from Canterbury reached the Vatican. Innocent III, one of the wisest and ablest of popes, did not stand in awe of King John of England. Nor was he to be hurried into a decision as to whether Reginald or John Grey was the rightful Archbishop of Canterbury. He announced that he must make a careful study of the Church laws regarding such elections before deciding.

As he debated the question in his mind, it occurred to him that he had among his cardinals the very man to become archbishop. It was advisable that such a man have experience in the administration of the Church, which could best be obtained in Rome. He must command the respect and good will of the bishops and other churchmen in England. Innocent III knew what kind of man John was, yet if the new archbishop were to succeed, he must work in harmony with the King, and at the same time be strong enough not to be intimidated.

Considering the matter, the Pope reached the conclusion that the man about whom he was thinking had all these abilities. He announced that neither of the two claimants had been legally chosen. Reginald's election, having been conducted in secret, was not valid. Neither was John Grey's, since it had taken place before the first election had been annulled by Rome.

Innocent III then sent to Canterbury the name of the man he recommended. When the new election was held, Stephen Cardinal Langton was chosen Archbishop of Canterbury.

John's rage when he learned of Reginald's election was like a tiny whirlwind of dust compared to the tempest which fairly rocked the foundations of his palace of Westminster when he heard that Stephen Langton was archbishop. He dispatched two knights galloping full tilt to Canterbury, where they burst into the monastery with drawn swords.

"In the name of the King, leave England instantly, or we will set this place afire and roast you all alive!" they shouted.

The terrified prior and his monks fled to Flanders, and John seized the substantial revenues of Canterbury for himself.

Three English bishops came to Westminster. "His Holiness the Pope has ordered us to call upon you, Sire," one said. "We are instructed to tell you he hopes you will be reasonable, but unless Stephen Cardinal Langton is accepted as Archbishop of Canterbury he will place all England under an interdict."

At these words the King was filled with such fury it seemed he might hurl himself upon the three prelates and tear them to pieces. He cursed Innocent III and all the members of the College of Cardinals.

"Let the Pope try it!" he shrieked. "Tell your master in Rome that if he dares do so we will drive every last bishop, priest and friar out of our kingdom, and seize all the property of the Church! We will even hunt down your clerks, and gouge out the eyes and slit the nostrils of everyone we lay hands on! Let your master issue a thousand interdicts if he pleases!"

Innocent III retaliated with the interdict. He did not expect to have to keep it in force for long, since it was a powerful instrument, and the influence of the Church in England was great. To the humble people of the kingdom, the interdict was a catastrophe. The churches were closed. No masses could be said, and no Holy Communion given. Dying persons could not receive extreme unction, and the ground in which the dead were buried could not be consecrated. Those who married no longer received the blessing of the Church. To these poor people the interdict took away their very hope of salvation.

But John, who was no godly man, was not at all disturbed. In fact, he was delighted to have an excuse for seizing all the vast landholdings of the Church in England.

As for his barons, the majority were on his side, believing the Pope had no right to interfere in the selection of an Archbishop of Canterbury. And those who did not agree dared do nothing about it. In this beginning of King John's long quarrel with the Church, he was the victor. The losers were the Church in England and the wretched common people, who were devout in their Catholic faith.

Yet indirectly the interdict did have a powerful effect upon the King. Even though most of the barons supported him in his quarrel with the Church, John's nature was so suspicious that he became convinced they were plotting to overthrow him. Probably he had heard false tales circulated by enemies and mischief-makers. He tried to put the stories out of his mind, but they persisted in tormenting him.

John was afraid, and a man in a panic of fear will do senseless and unreasoning things. This was as cruel a ruler as ever sat on the throne of England, and one of the meanest and most grasping. He thought that by striking at the barons with the weapons of his cruelty and avarice he could frighten them into obedience. Instead, the very hostility he mistakenly believed existed among them gradually did arise.

3

Since Stephen Langton had not dared come to England to assume his duties, he was sent to a monastery in France where seventy of the Canterbury monks had taken refuge. Then, about the year 1209, he received an assignment which pleased him greatly when he was chosen as chancellor of his alma mater, the University of Paris.

While he was there, many clergymen and others who either had aroused the King's displeasure or could no longer bear to live under the interdict and had fled the country, came to Langton seeking refuge or guidance. Among them was a group of students from Oxford. Although the famous English university was then in the earliest years of its existence, it was already flourishing.

From these young men the archbishop heard a story which gravely disturbed him.

"Why did you leave England?" he asked them.

"Because we could no longer remain in a country where

30

one cannot obtain justice under the law, my Lord Archbishop," replied their spokesman. "When some of our fellow students were hanged for a murder they did not commit, we came to France."

"Murder! . . . hanged?" gasped the prelate.

"One of the students killed a woman. It was an accident, but fearing he would be given no chance to prove it, he fled from England. The mayor of Oxford was determined to have someone punished, and he ordered the sheriff of Oxfordshire to seize several students who had had nothing to do with the woman's death, and put them in jail."

"You are certain of their innocence?"

"Yes, your Eminence."

"Were they brought to trial?"

"Before the King himself. Being in the vicinity when the itinerant justices of the royal court held their sessions in Oxford, he sat with them, as he so often does, when the case was tried in the shire hall. The tyrant ordered the young men hanged on the spot."

"God's mercy!" cried Langton. "Could they not prove their innocence?"

"They were given no chance! The only evidence allowed was that of the mayor, who charged they had deliberately killed the woman."

Stephen Langton reflected long on what the young men had told him. He was reluctant to think it had happened just as they said, yet he had been impressed by their earnestness. Before long he heard other tales which shocked and angered him, and did nothing to improve his respect for the King.

John had already begun the persecutions and wrongs that in time were to bring about his undoing. In the very year of 1209, in which Stephen Langton is believed to have taken his seat as chancellor of the University of Paris, the King issued a cruel order which fell heavily, not only upon certain barons, but with even more devastating force upon the wretched peasants of their manors.

John was fond of hunting and often stayed for a time in one of his castles within the vast royal forests which covered much of England in medieval days. Some of these were no more than large hunting lodges, since they were unfortified. There the King hunted deer and other animals, accompanied by the barons and knights of the royal household.

Next to fighting, the chief accomplishment of a nobleman in England was to be a great hunter. While the royal forests were reserved for the King's use, lords of manors and their knights were also allowed to hunt in them under certain limitations. But the common people, who also loved hunting and could well have used the meat of these wild animals to eke out their scanty fare, were strictly forbidden to hunt under severe penalties.

A royal forest was not all woodland. Within its boundaries were open or cleared areas in which stood villages and the fields and meadows farmed by the inhabitants as vassals of a manor lord. They lived under a whole set of special laws which applied to the royal forests. The one forbidding them to hunt was not the worst of the privations these poor country people suffered, however.

The forest laws were administered by a high government official known as the chief forester. Under him, in each royal forest, was a warden heading a force of foresters who roamed the woodlands seeking poachers and other law violators. The wardens were favorites of the King, rewarded by him with these posts, which gave them great power. Many used that

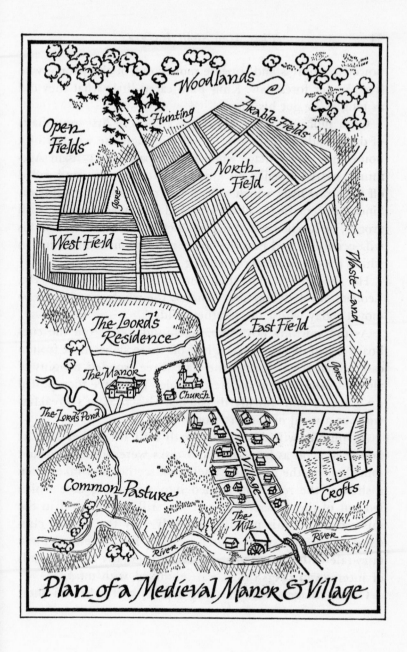

Plan of a Medieval Manor & Village

power to oppress and squeeze money out of the people who lived under forest law. King John cared little what they did as long as he got his share.

On a morning in early July of 1209, the first gray shafts of dawn had barely begun to steal through the window of a house in a rural village when its occupant, the peasant Agemund, stirred, opened his eyes, stretched drowsily and rolled off the straw litter which was his bed on the hard earth floor. Since he slept in his clothes he did not have to dress. Still groggy, he lurched out of the small chamber which he and his wife occupied, and into the larger main room of his house in which his two sons were sleeping.

He shook first one, then the other. "Up, Walter! Up, Leofric! No dallying, now! There's the whole meadow to be mown today whilst the weather holds."

As the yawning boys rose, Agemund took from the cupboard a loaf of bread, wrenched off three slabs, drew from a cask which stood against the wall three wooden noggins of ale, and placed all on the trestle table. The three then pulled up a bench and quickly dispatched this peasant's breakfast without a word of conversation.

Agemund's wife Alice was already astir when they left the house; as soon as her household tasks were done she would join them in the hayfield. They took scythes and rakes from a shed at the rear, and turned into a winding lane which led out of the village. The sun was still not up, and in the misty dawn of this morning in early July the houses, clustered about the stone church, looked like a setting for a fairy tale with their thatched roofs and roughly finished walls of interwoven twigs called wattle, mixed with mud.

Other villagers, also carrying scythes and rakes on their

shoulders, were leaving their dwellings and trudging down the lane. Like Agemund and his sons they were barefoot and wore short tunics or blouses of coarse homespun nearly the color of the soil they tilled, ankle-length breeches cross-laced about the legs with thongs, and flat-brimmed hats.

As Agemund and the boys passed a stone crucifix by the wayside, they crossed themselves, then plodded on and at length turned into a meadow. The sun had just burst over a low ridge to the east. Agemund took off his hat and mopped his forehead with his arm.

" 'Twill be hot," he said. "Goodly haying weather."

He stopped, and for a moment stood looking out over the fields and meadows which stretched in all directions on both sides of the road. The land was divided into sections, some of it meadow and pasture, some tilled land, some lying fallow until the next season. Each section was a peasant's grant. The portions of the tract in which crops had been sown were surrounded by ditches and thick whitethorn hedges. These kept out not only the sheep, pigs and cattle, but the deer and other wild animals of the King's forest of Essex which rose like a green wall not far to the westward.

"A good summer for the crops too." Agemund pointed to a field which adjoined the meadow. "See how tall our wheat has already grown. If God is good to us"—he crossed himself again—"we shall have a fine harvest."

They set to work then, Agemund and Walter moving abreast down the field, swinging their scythes in practiced rhythm. Each "swish!" of the long blades cut a wide swath in the tall grass. Behind them Leofric, the younger lad, raked the sweet-smelling hay into long windrows.

Two hours passed. The three peasants worked silently,

stopping only to wipe the sweat from their faces as the bur-
nished sun rose higher and beat down upon them with ever
greater intensity.

Suddenly Leofric stopped raking. "Father!" he cried,
"what is that?"

The scythes halted as the other two looked in the direction
in which Leofric pointed. There, at the far edge of their
wheatfield, smoke was rising.

"Fire!" Agemund shouted. "The hedge is afire!"

As he spoke, orange flames burst out of the swirling smoke.
All three threw down their implements and raced toward
the burning hedge. Approaching it, they saw men moving
about, lifting dry faggots and brush from a cart and piling
them against the greenery of the hedge.

"It is the warden and his foresters!" panted Agemund.
"They are setting fires all along our hedge! And look!—
some of his men are filling up the ditch!"

Once he had come face to face with the forest warden,
Agemund's servility struck him dumb. He was only a poor
villein; how could he demand why the warden was carrying
out this destruction? This was a King's officer, as powerful
in his realm of Essex Forest as a sheriff in his shire.

Other peasants had seen the fire from their meadows, however, and were running in from all directions. One, Ralf,
a freeman and a person of some consequence in the village,
was bolder.

"For God's sake, forbear, I pray you!" he cried. "Why do
your men set fire to the hedge of Agemund and level his
ditch? Dost not know 'twill allow the cattle and the beasts
from the forest to come in and eat his crops?"

The warden scowled, and his reply, spoken with a strong

French accent, was surly: "How now, sirrah? Who are you to question the actions of a King's officer? Go back to your work."

"Dost intend to destroy all our hedges and ditches?" Ralf persisted.

"All," snapped the warden. And as a chorus of growls and mutterings arose from the dismayed peasants, he added, "I told you to get back to your work! Begone! or—" He advanced a step toward them, and his hand flew to the hilt of the sword at his girdle.

The farmers fell back in alarm. Their leader, Ralf, made a gesture with his head. "Let us go away as he says," he told them softly, "and decide what is to be done about this."

He led the angry men into the meadow where he had been mowing. Once they were out of the warden's hearing, others found their tongues.

"Let us charge him and his men and stop them!" one cried.

"Nay," said Ralf, "for 'twould do us no good. Dost want to swing from a rope's end on the gallows, or spend the rest of thy life in prison?"

"Better that than to starve," said another man. "There will be little enough left of our grain by harvest time if we do nought."

"A murrain on all the Frenchmen who are among the King's officers!" growled a freeman. "They are the worst of the lot. This fellow is not satisfied to fill his purse by summoning us into court and fining us for things we have not done, but he must enrich himself still further by forcing us to pay high prices for the bad ale he brews. Why didn't he stay in France where he belongs?"

"We will go to the manor house and talk to the lord,"

Ralf decided. "He will not let us suffer this injustice. Besides, how can we pay him for the use of his land if we have no crops?"

The more clearheaded of the peasants promptly nodded in agreement, while those who had been in favor of more drastic action were soon convinced the freeman was right. With Ralf leading them, they all stalked out of the meadow and back up the road to the village.

When they had trooped through it they approached the manor house just beyond. They crossed a drawbridge over its moat, passed through a gate in the earthen wall which surrounded it, and entered the courtyard of the manor. Around its edge stood the bakehouse, brewery, laundry, stables and the manor house itself, its great hall built of stone and the lord's living quarters above it of timber.

The lord of the manor had ridden in just ahead of them, it appeared, for his splendid horse and those of several knights who had accompanied him were being led away to the stables by grooms.

The lord himself, a tall, commanding figure wearing a riding costume with its knee-length tunic of brown, and a mantle and peaked cap, both of forest green, was surrounded by a group of his employes. All were talking and gesticulating at once. Among them the peasants recognized his steward, bailiff, foreman, reeve and hayward.

The peasants, halted at the edge of the courtyard, saw the lord fling his hands over his head and heard him shout, "I can do nothing, I tell you!" Then, followed by his knights, he strode into the great hall.

Since the reeve was a peasant like themselves, elected by them to assist the lord's bailiff in overseeing the running of the manor farm, the group approached him. Their spokesman, Ralf, blurted out what had happened.

"We know the lord will help us!" he cried. "We must see him, Godric!"

"Help you!" the reeve snorted. "Look over there!"

The peasants' eyes followed his pointing finger, and their mouths fell open. There in the distance, where the lands of the manor farm approached the forest, smoke was also rising.

"How can he help you when his own hedges are afire, and his ditches being leveled?" the reeve continued. "Didst not hear him say he could do nought?"

"What means this, Godric?" one of the peasants demanded.

"The lord said only that it is being done by the King's order. Early this morning, when I went with the hayward and some of the villeins to mow the lord's meadow as he ordered before he left for London, the forest warden and his men were there, setting fire to the hedges. When I told the warden the lord would be angry, he only laughed. That is all I can tell you."

A wail went up from the peasants. "What are we to do?" one cried.

"Don't we stand enough?" a freeman shouted. "We must not only go to all the sessions of the manor court, but we are ordered to attend the forest courts as well because we are told it is the King's law. Or, if we do not wish to miss a day's work, we must pay a fine for being absent. The oftener the warden holds court, the poorer we get, whilst he lines his pockets with silver. And now this! Where will it end?"

Agemund recovered his voice at last. "What about the laws that forbid us to hunt in the forest, and even fine us for trespass there? Or if we are caught owning a hunting dog, or bow and arrows? And God help the poor poacher who is caught taking a deer to give his hungry family a bit of venison!"

"Aye!" chimed in another villein, "why should we not hunt in the forest of Essex? There is plenty of game for all— red and fallow deer, roe, wild boar, hares, squirrels. If we all refused to obey the forest laws—"

"Better keep thy tongue in thy head, Ailwin," warned the reeve, "or thou mayst lose them both. If such talk reached the King's ears. . . . As for what is happening to the hedges and ditches, you will all be wise to make the best of it, for there is nought else you can do."

Since it had been made plain that the lord could not help them, the peasants had to take the reeve's advice. Still muttering, wearing long faces, they shambled back to their fields.

Inside the manor house, the lord had left his knights in the great hall while he went to his private quarters. There his wife Rosamund greeted him in great distress over the actions of the forest warden and his men.

"I cannot understand it, William!" she cried. "Why should the King do this? You have always enjoyed his favor. Did you see him in London?"

Her husband flung himself into a chair. The Lady Rosamund saw that he looked tired and worn. "Aye, my dear," he replied. "It seems that I have fallen from favor. . . ."

"And that is why he is trying to ruin us by destroying the hedges and ditches?"

"We did not discuss that," said the lord. "But I heard from others of the royal household that he plans a journey to his lodge in the forest later in the summer for some hunting. It is said that he ordered this thing done so the forest animals will be fat for his larder when he arrives. But that was not why I was summoned to Westminster, my dear."

"What was it, then?"

"He demands I surrender Peter to him as a hostage"—the lord shook his head grimly, and his voice was bitter as he added, "for my good behavior."

His wife uttered a shriek. "No! No, William! I will not let him take my son!"

"We must," her husband replied. "Peter will be safe enough . . . provided nothing happens to raise the King's suspicions further. . . ."

"Suspicions!" she cried. "What does he suspect?"

"That I am plotting against him, or so I was told. He himself gave no reason."

"But why? Why? You have always been loyal."

The lord rose from his chair and began to pace the floor, his forehead creased with worry. "Verily I know not!" he burst out. "They told me in London that since his quarrel with the Church began, the King no longer trusts any of his barons. Of what he has heard to make him suspect me, I have no idea, save that it is false!"

Other barons, he told her, had received like demands that their sons be given into the King's keeping as hostages so that he could kill them if their fathers turned against him.

"If I refuse," he said, "he will hound us into fleeing the kingdom, seize the manor and its lands, and brand me an outlaw so that if we ever return, anyone can kill me and claim a reward."

Since he had no other choice, he sent his son to join the royal household as one of King John's knights. The reeve Godric had been wrong in saying the lord could do nothing to help the peasants, however, for he organized them to patrol the tilled lands, though they were so extensive that it was impossible to drive off all the domestic and forest animals which wandered upon them. Nevertheless, they were able to preserve a substantial part of the crop.

Then, one day near harvest time in late August, the peasants, hard at work in their fields, stopped and looked up at the sound of a coachman's horn. A cloud of dust swirled up from the road. Ahead of it they saw a ponderous coach jolting over the ruts and potholes of the highway leading toward the forest. It was closed in by an arched canopy and drawn by eight richly caparisoned horses in tandem. The peasants heard the coachman crack his whip, saw the postilions leaning forward, perched on their horses' backs.

From mouth to mouth the word spread through the fields: "The King! There is the King—the one on the great white horse ahead of the coach—on his way to his hunting lodge!"

The peasants gaped at the spectacle. Through a window in its side and the open end of the royal coach, they vaguely glimpsed the costumes of gaily dressed, titled ladies riding inside. Among them was Isabella, John's young queen, with her two small sons—Henry, the heir apparent to the throne, who was not yet two years old, and the baby, Prince Richard. Ahead, with the King, and behind the coach cantered many armed and brilliantly costumed knights, some with their ladies on pillions behind their saddles.

Trailing in the wake of the cavalcade was a motley train of pack animals and carts loaded with baggage and with clerks, butlers, stewards, cooks, dispensers, cupbearers, slaughterers, bakers, laundresses, chamberlains and other servants of the household, as well as the buffoons, mountebanks and minstrels who entertained the court. Among the carts was one loaded with the King's fine feather bed and its coverings of linen and rugs.

The faces of the peasants were apathetic as they gazed after the receding procession. In order that King John and his household might enjoy the finest venison, the winter ahead for these wretched people would be a hard one, with provisions scant because of the smaller harvest, and the specter of debt haunting them. Yet they knew they could do nothing about it.

Nor did it occur to them to envy the knights and ladies of the King's train for the luxury in which they lived, for these nobility were of a world as remote from their own as the moon and stars. A peasant's life was always filled with hardship; it had been so in their fathers' and grandfathers' time, and would be so forever, no doubt.

Their apathy was jolted into consternation the next day by the sound of the huntsman's horn and the baying of hounds.

Then they saw first a red deer in full flight, the dogs close at his heels, followed by the King and twoscore mounted knights in furious pursuit. The frantic animal sped through one wheatfield after another before making a wide sweep and heading back toward the forest from which it had come.

The stunned peasants saw the tall, full-headed stalks of waving wheat go down, trampled under the thudding hoofs of the horses. The destruction took only moments before the hunters disappeared over a rise in the land, leaving behind them desolation, ruin and despair.

4

John's cruel forest decree had fallen upon only a small group of villagers and their manor lord, but Innocent III's interdict distressed all of the devout common people in Catholic England. As time went on and the King showed no signs of yielding, the Pope determined to strike directly at him in order to bring him to terms.

He issued a decree of excommunication. It meant that the monarch was no longer a member of the Church, and was damned to burn in hell. All Catholics were forbidden to have anything to do with him or to give him shelter, food or drink.

Hopeful, however, that a settlement of the quarrel might yet be reached, the Pope ordered the pronouncement held in abeyance until Stephen Langton might decide it should be published. A series of negotiations with John was then begun.

In his fear that the barons were plotting against him and would have the people's support in a rebellion, John realized that the Church of Rome would be a powerful ally of his enemies in such a struggle. He was willing to make peace, but only upon his own terms. At last, in the fall of 1209, Stephen Langton, acting at the Pope's instructions, crossed the English Channel under a safe-conduct issued by the King, expecting to meet him at Dover. Instead two royal envoys appeared.

"Is your master ready to accept me as Archbishop of Canterbury?" Langton asked.

"Yes," they told him, "providing an agreement on his terms can be reached."

"And will he restore all the lands he has seized from the Church?"

The emissaries knew John had no intention of giving back all the Church property, with its rich revenues. They gave the cardinal an evasive answer: "Some of them . . . perhaps."

Langton soon saw that an agreement acceptable to the Church could not be reached, and he returned to Paris. Thereupon he had the excommunication published in France, though no English churchman dared do so. Again, in the spring of 1210, the cardinal was heartened when John sent two English clergymen to talk peace with him. But the King's terms had not changed, and nothing came of the discussion.

Meanwhile, John was occupied with troubles of another kind. Rebellion was stirring among the belligerent and restless people of Ireland, never content to be ruled by a foreign monarch. He decided to invade his wild domains there, and set about raising a great army and assembling seven hundred ships to transport it across the Irish Sea.

At the same time he resolved to settle an old score with an enemy who had once been one of his intimate companions.

Difficulties having arisen between them in 1208, soon after publication of the interdict, John had acted with swift malevolence against this old friend, William de Briouse.

His persecutions had reached a climax one day in that year when his royal court was sitting in Westminster Hall, a part of his great palace of Westminster in London.

The weather was chill and dreary, and the hall was dim in the gray light which fell through its narrow, roundheaded windows as the court began its session that day. The only other illumination came from a fire which blazed on the open hearth, but failed dismally to relieve the gloom.

A bailiff rose and called out: "Oyez! Oyez! Oyez! All persons having business before the Court of the King's Bench draw near."

Having opened the court, he turned toward the judges in their scarlet robes, seated on a high dais below the great arched roof overhead. In the center, on a chair elevated slightly above the rest, sat a man dressed in regal splendor. That day, as he so often did, King John was presiding over his royal court. He nodded to the bailiff.

"William de Briouse, Baron of Bramber and Barnstaple, Lord of Abergavenny, Brecon and Limerick, come forward!" cried the court officer.

There was a stir and a craning of necks among the spectators in the gallery. From an enclosure in front of the dais, a man in the black robe of a sergeant-at-law stood up, came before the judges and knelt. At a signal from the King, he rose and spoke: "Sire, your baron and vassal, William de Briouse, is ill and unable to appear."

John fixed the lawyer with a black scowl. "Curse him and his illness! He is never too ill for knavery. We accepted in good faith the surrender of his castles on the Marches of

Wales in payment of his debt to us for granting him the lord-ship of Limerick. Having thus acquitted himself, he turned like a jackal and attacked the strongholds, thinking to repossess them."

The sergeant-at-law bowed humbly. "I pray your pardon, my liege, but if such a report has reached your ears, you have been misinformed. The Baron de Briouse has made no attempt to regain the castles he surrendered to you."

It was apparent to those in the courtroom that the King was about to fly into one of his tempestuous rages. He fixed the sergeant-at-law with a piercing gaze, his face darkened and his body began to bob up and down, as though he might at any moment launch himself and leap down upon the attorney.

"Do you presume to stand before us and deny what we have told you?" he thundered.

"N-no, my liege," the man stammered. "It is only that information of the most reliable nature—"

"Hold!" the King screamed. "Whatever Briouse told you is a lie! This vassal of ours is not to be trusted."

"I pray you, Sire, to believe he is loyal and obedient to your will. . . ."

"He plots against us! That is why we demanded that his sons be surrendered to us as hostages for his good behavior. Mayhap you would like to deny that when our officers went to his stronghold to take them into custody, his wife refused to deliver up the young men. She had the insolence to accuse us of . . ."

The King stopped, reconsidering what he had been about to say, but it was plain that the memory of what the Baroness de Briouse had told his officers was unpleasant.

"She was indiscreet, Sire," the lawyer murmured. "The

Baron de Briouse rebuked her and, as you know, offered to appear before the royal court to be judged for any offense he might have committed."

"Then where is he?" the King raged. "Tell us that!"

The attorney opened his mouth to speak, then closed it and said nothing.

"You claim this vassal is obedient to our will," John continued. "Then explain to us why, when we directed that his goods at Limerick in our domain of Ireland be seized in satisfaction of his debt, our officers there found he had removed them. And why did he resist our men who sought to seize his goods at his strongholds on the Marches?"

Again the sergeant-at-law could not or dared not reply.

John's gaze swerved and fastened itself upon the clerk of the court, busily plying his quill as he strove to scribble down all that had been said. "Draw up an order to state that the Baron de Briouse, having been three times summoned before our court as directed by law, and having failed to appear, all his lands and goods are forfeit to the Crown, and that he is adjudged outlawed by default."

The King turned to the justices. "Is this your judgment?"

They nodded meekly.

Again John addressed the clerk: "Let our order be sent to the sheriffs of all counties in our domains, to be published to all therein resident. Let it further state that a reward of two marks will be paid to any person who shall bring the head of our vassal Briouse to Westminster."

The King's malignant eyes swept over all who were in the Hall of Westminster, and they quailed before it.

"Let William de Briouse bear the wolf's-head!" he shouted.

The sun had set and twilight was deepening over the coast of northern Ireland one day some two years later when a large boat made its way from sea into the Lough of Belfast. The lookout in the craft's boxlike forecastle perched on the upcurved end of its prow could scarcely see the outlines of Carrickfergus Castle's towers and walls as he guided the man at the steering oar in approaching the rocky tongue of land jutting into the bay.

The boat had been seen from the castle, however. When its sail was lowered and its keel grated on the beach, dark figures, silhouetted in the dusk by rushlight torches, hurried toward the newcomers. The one in the lead, a tall broad-shouldered man, whose suit of ring mail gleamed in the flaring light beneath his surcoat, reached the shore just as one of the men in the boat was assisting a lady to disembark.

"Matilda!" he cried, embracing her. "It is you! Forgive my warlike appearance, my dear lady, but from the battlements in the gathering darkness my men could not be certain that your boat's approach did not herald the arrival of an armed force."

The Baroness de Briouse was a stately figure in the torchlight. "We are grateful to see armed men of whom we do not have to fear for our lives," she replied. "We have been in terror lest we lose them. It was the approach of the King and his army that forced us to flee from your brother Walter's castle of Meath."

"Ah," said Hugh de Lacy, Earl of Ulster, "I have heard of the King's expedition against his rebellious subjects here in Ireland. I trust that my brother and your charming daughter, his wife, are safe, and that the castle may be defended against the invaders."

"Whether it will stand I do not know." Anxiety edged Matilda's voice. "Your brother insisted that we leave before the King's army arrived, since your castle is the stronger."

"When we are within it you shall tell me more of this," said her host. And when she had presented the others of her party—her sons William and John, their wives and several of her grandchildren—he added, "You are all welcome to Carrickfergus. Let us delay no longer, for I am sure you are tired and hungry after your voyage."

The boat's crew were dragging it up on the shore. Lacy spoke to one of his servants: "See that these men are given meat and lodging in the servants' hall."

Taking the Baroness de Briouse by the arm, he led the way over the path which edged the castle walls and rounded the promontory. A gate between two towers at the landward end swung open at the party's approach.

Passing through it, they crossed a drawbridge spanning the moat, and went through another arched gateway into the main courtyard. Before them a second wall barred off the great square keep which towered high above them. When they reached the barrier, a wooden stairway was lowered on ropes; they ascended it, entered the keep, climbed a spiral stone staircase to its third story and came into the great hall of the castle.

It was a scene of barbaric splendor. The hall, rising two full stories to the heavily timbered roof of the keep, was gloomy. Candles, made from rushes dipped in melted fat, shed only a dim and flickering light. In strange contrast, the varicolored costumes of Earl Hugh de Lacy's knights and their ladies stood out through the dimness. To add to the wildness of the setting, hawks on perches fastened to the walls looked down upon the company with fierce eyes. Hounds, also used in the chase, lolled at ease on the rush-strewn floor, licking their chops in anticipation at the smell of roasting meat wafted up from the kitchen on the floor below the hall.

The household had been sitting down to the evening meal when the sentinels on the battlements reported the boat's approach. Now, as the earl and his visitors came in, a hush fell over the hall, and all eyes were fixed in curiosity upon Matilda de Briouse and her party.

In the Baroness de Briouse they beheld a handsome woman, past middle age, whose face betrayed the strain of her flight. Her robe, as she laid aside her dark blue mantle, bore the marks of wear and rough travel, though it was of fine, heavy stuff, white, with a pattern of golden crescents, and brocaded with woven threads of gold. On her head she wore a white linen wimple covered by a stiffened round turban of the same material.

Lacy ushered the guests to his table raised on a dais and, when they were seated, put up his hand for silence. He was a craggy, bold-eyed man with the face of one accustomed to fighting for whatever he achieved. After he had introduced the visitors, an excited buzz spread through the hall when he explained the reason for the party's departure from the castle of Baron Walter de Lacy in Meath.

As he took his seat, a servant handed around a basin filled with water, and a towel, and all at the high table washed their hands. Cupbearers were serving ale in pewter cups. The earl lifted his high. "To your safe refuge in Carrickfergus!" he pledged the newcomers, and all raised theirs and drank. Turning to the baroness, he said, "Tell me, my dear Matilda, how you came to leave England, and what has befallen you since. In this remote place we seldom hear news of home."

"It is a long story, my Lord Hugh," she replied. "As you may know, William fell from the royal grace some two years ago when he was unable to make payment of five thousand marks the King had demanded for conferring the lordship of Limerick upon him. Since then his Majesty has hounded him. . . ."

"Ah, yes," said Lacy, "the King would like to do the same to me and your son-in-law, my brother. It was fortunate that we were able to defeat him and his army here in Ireland in 1205, and force him to grant us the lands we now hold, as well as make me an earl and Walter a baron. Until now, he has never since dared try to overthrow us. What form did his persecutions take?"

"First, a demand that our sons be surrendered as hostages for payment of the debt. I confronted the King's men when they came, and refused to deliver them up."

"What reason did you give?"

Looking at his visitor, the earl saw her mouth set firmly before she replied, "I told them I would never yield my sons to the murderer of Arthur of Brittany!"

"By my hilt!" cried Lacy, "you were bold, dear lady!"

"I spoke the truth. I cannot tell you the story, my Lord Hugh, for my husband swore me to secrecy. Being then high in the royal favor, he was with the King in France when Arthur was imprisoned. He is the only man in England besides the King who knows how the lad met his end. But I can tell you this: the murder rests upon his Majesty's head!"

"I think that is well known to everyone," said her host.

Meanwhile, servingmen had entered bearing great platters of bread, and placed slices of it before each person; then followed a procession of others carrying slabs of roasted venison, each impaled upon a spit. These they laid on the bread. More ale was served, and the company fell to, using their knives to hack off pieces of meat, and their fingers to convey them to their mouths. A harper appeared and sang romantic ballads while he plucked the strings of his instrument.

While she and the rest ate, Matilda resumed her story. "The King first tried to have William's goods at the castle in Limerick seized, but William was able to have them taken away in time and hidden. Since he acknowledges his debt to the Crown, however, he surrendered his castles on the Marches of Wales. The King was not satisfied, and summoned William to appear before his court at Westminster."

"Your husband went?"

"He would have gone if he had not known the King would seize him if he did. He was summoned three times to the court. . . ."

Hugh de Lacy nodded. "And then the King outlawed him?"

"Exactly, my Lord Hugh."

"Aye," mused the earl, "it is his favorite way of taking revenge upon his enemies. Your husband is not the first of John's barons to bear the wolf's-head, you know, nor will he be the last. And this, I presume, made your flight from England necessary?"

"Yes," said the baroness, "we escaped to Ireland and took refuge with William Marshal, Earl of Pembroke, in Leinster."

Lacy nodded in understanding. "You could rely upon his protection since, like your husband, he is one of the King's intimates who has fallen from grace. John was ill-advised to let some petty disagreement cause an estrangement with one so loyal to him."

"The King seems to have realized it," said Matilda. "When he decided to invade Ireland, he summoned the earl to join his army."

"And Marshal obeyed?"

"Yes, but before that he refused to deliver us up when John's justiciar in Ireland tried to seize us. Instead he sent us under an escort to your brother's castle in Meath."

Their conversation was interrupted by a great hubbub of snarls and howls in the hall. Two of the dogs were fighting over a bone flung to them by one of the knights. Servants grabbed the animals, pulled them apart, and with well-placed kicks sent them slinking from the hall with their tails between their legs.

"Where is your husband now?" the earl asked when the excitement had died down.

"After we arrived in Meath he decided to return to Wales in the hope of resolving his quarrel with the King."

"Indeed," said Lacy, "and do you know whether he has had any success?"

"The King refused even to hear his proposals as long as I remained at liberty."

The earl looked grave. "And I fear he will not listen until he has had his revenge. He never forgets an injury, and your accusation must have touched him in a sore spot. You will do well to stay out of his clutches, my dear Matilda. And William is still in Wales?"

"Yes, he has had some success in regaining the lands seized by the King under the decree of outlawry. He has raised a force which caused John to send soldiers against him."

"The King may yet regret this," said Lacy. "A bold outlaw like your husband can cause him great trouble."

The Baroness de Briouse sighed. "Perhaps . . . but I live in fear that William may be captured. . . ."

"Take heart, Matilda. It may turn out as it did when his Majesty outlawed Fulk FitzWarin, and the knight organized a daring band who like himself bore the wolf's-head. Surely you have heard how he and his followers led John a merry chase through all the forests of England, preying on the royal lands, and at last forcing the King to revoke the decree of outlawry and restore Fulk's property. Your husband, too, is a dauntless man. . . ."

The meal was nearly over. Cups of spiced wine were being served, and once more the bowl of water and the towel were passed around the high table.

"A strolling band of acrobats and jugglers arrived this afternoon," said the earl. "If you are not too tired, perhaps you will join us in watching their performance."

Matilda de Briouse smiled wearily. "I am sure the younger ones will enjoy it, but if you will forgive me, I should like to rest." A look of apprehension crossed her face. "Do you think we shall be safe here, my Lord Hugh?"

"We can only wait and see," said Lacy slowly. "I shall send out some of my knights to see what they can learn of the King's attempt upon my brother's castle. Should he succeed in taking it, he will surely move north and lay siege to Carrickfergus. The castle is strong, but we have neither enough knights and soldiers to meet his host in battle, nor provisions to withstand a long siege. Whatever happens, you shall have my full protection, dear lady."

Late one afternoon several days later, the castle was thrown into a turmoil when the earl's riders thundered into the courtyard, dismounted from their sweating horses and an-

nounced that King John had captured the stronghold of
Meath and was marching north.

Hugh de Lacy summoned Matilda. "The King's strength
is very great," he told her. "Resistance would only waste the
lives of my knights and men in prolonging our inevitable
surrender. I have ordered the castle abandoned. Most of my
household will find safety in one of the other lordships of my
domain of Ulster, but I dare not risk letting you go with
them. You and your family must seek a more distant refuge."

"But whither, my Lord Hugh?" cried the baroness. "How
can we escape the King?"

"The voyage to Scotland is not a long one. Your boat is
staunch and fitted for the passage, and I, with a few of my
best knights, will go with you. King William, the Lion of
Scotland, is no friend of his Majesty's, for only last year when
John invaded his realm he was forced to accept a humiliating
peace. If we can reach Edinburgh you will find safe refuge."

There was no time to be lost. Matilda, her sons and their
families assembled their scanty belongings and the following
day embarked once more in the boat, accompanied by the
earl and his party. The wind and weather were fair, and by
early afternoon they were nearing the Scottish coast.

"We will steer north into the Firth of Clyde," Lacy told
the baroness, "and ascend the river Clyde as far as possible.
Then we will make our way overland to Edinburgh."

But as the day waned, the weather became threatening.
"It will be best if we can find some shelter ashore for the
night," the earl decided.

The coast appeared to offer no refuge. Those in the boat
saw a bleak and forbidding shore with surf bursting in fury
over it, while beyond lay only mountains and trackless wilderness.

Night was beginning to shut down when at last the lookout shouted, "A castle! There!—on that neck of land."

The rest, straining their eyes, made out the castle, perched high on the rock of the promontory, its towers gray and ominous in the gloom.

"Steer for it," Lacy ordered. "There should be a place where we can land."

All were glad when the boat reached the lee of the promontory and the waves subsided somewhat. When it was fast to the shore, young William de Briouse and his mother were the first to disembark. Together they started over a rocky path leading to the castle on its elevation above them.

Part way up they halted and looked back to make sure the others were following. In that instant each was seized from behind and pinioned in the grip of several wild-looking men armed with broadswords. Scores of others, pouring from the castle's gateway, rushed by them and hurled themselves at the party on the shore.

The startled earl and his knights gave battle, but several were immediately struck down by the superior force of Scots, and it was plain that the rest must be overwhelmed.

"Fly!" Matilda screamed. "Save the others of my family!"

Realizing the hopelessness of his situation, Hugh de Lacy obeyed. Matilda and William had time only to see the boat push off and disappear in the dusk before they were dragged on up the path and into the castle.

Their captors spoke the strange, wild Gaelic language, but in the great hall of Turnberry Castle, where they were brought before its laird, Duncan, Earl of Carrick, one of his household was found who spoke a little French, as most of the English nobility did.

In Duncan of Carrick, Matilda and William saw nothing

to inspire hope, for his burly figure and cruel features held no pity, only ruthlessness. Like many Scottish lairds, most of his time was spent battling for supremacy with others in the ceaseless feuds between the clans of the mountain fastnesses.

By threats and menacing gestures, and with the help of the interpreter, Duncan soon badgered his captives' story from them. His ferocious eyes gleamed when he learned they were fugitives from the avenging hand of John, for he knew the English king would pay well for such a prize. He barked a terse order in Gaelic, and the two were hauled away and cast into one of the black dungeons of the keep.

The next morning Duncan sent a boat across the strait to Carrickfergus, which John and his army had seized. Some days later, the baroness and her son were taken from their dungeon and brought down to the shore.

Just off the promontory lay a good-sized ship flying the English flag, while a smaller boat waited at the landing place. There on the shore stood two iron cages, sent by John with two of his henchmen and a squad of crossbowmen. Matilda and William were locked into the cages and rowed out to the ship, which then spread its sail and set a course for England.

The boat containing Hugh de Lacy and the rest of the party had managed to find a safe haven for the night along that rock-bound coast, and in the morning they made their escape. In Wales, William de Briouse, in danger of being captured by the King's men, had also found safety by fleeing to France. But for Matilda de Briouse and young William, the ending was frightful.

At the King's order they were taken to Windsor Castle and imprisoned in one of its dungeons. A sheaf of oats and a flitch of raw bacon were flung in after them, and the door clanged shut.

That was the last food they ever received. They were then left to starve in the darkness of their foul prison. John of England had taken his terrible revenge.

5

With his powerful army, the King soon put down the rebellion in Ireland, capturing a number of castles and forcing more than a score of Irish chieftains to swear loyalty to him. Then, leaving a new justiciar to enforce his rule there, he hastily returned to England, for word had reached him of a new revolt in Wales, which he claimed as part of his domains, though actually he had little control over its unruly barons.

Before setting out for Wales he tarried in London long enough to summon to his palace of Westminster every archbishop, bishop and abbot who still remained in England. He knew that most of them had large sums of money in their care, revenues which had come in before he had seized the lands belonging to the Church, and which were used in carrying out its work. Moreover, from past financial records, known as pipe rolls and maintained by the Exchequer, he had a shrewd idea of just how much each had.

Picking out first this one, then that one, he bluntly told

them how much money he expected from each as a "gift."
They were helpless, for they knew if they refused he would
send officers to ransack their churches and abbeys, and then
drive them from the country. All paid the exorbitant sums
he demanded. With that, John marched for Wales.

Thus he was not present one day in 1211 to enjoy his diver-
sion of presiding over his royal court when it sat in a shire
town in England's Midlands. Housewives bound for market
that morning, and other citizens going about their business,
turned to look at three riders cantering through the main
street. They were stern-faced men, wearing long scarlet robes
beneath black mantles whose cowls were drawn over their
heads.

The riders drew up at the shire hall, dismounted and
tethered their horses. As they entered the hall a beadle cried,
"Rise! All rise for their worships, the itinerant justices of the
King's Court of Assize!"

While those in the crowded hall stood, the judges, who
were on their rounds of the counties of King John's realm,
advanced and took their seats on a dais at the far end of the
chamber. The rest then sat down, and with his cry of "Oyez!"
the beadle declared the court in session. The room was filled
with spectators, sergeants-at-law, bailiffs, clerks and other
court attachés.

The beadle then intoned, "Stand forth, Godiva Basset!"

A door at the end of the hall, which communicated with a
stairway leading to the dungeons below, swung open, and a
bailiff appeared leading a woman. He took her before the
judges' dais. The sheriff of the county then rose and came
forward.

"May it please your Worships," he began, "the woman
Godiva Basset, charged with arson, has appeared before me

during the regular session of the shire court, at which time a presentment was made, and a profession of innocence entered by the appellee. She was then held to await a plea of the Crown, since it was an appeal of felony."

"Who is the appellant in the case?" asked the presiding judge.

"Hawisa Turpin, your Worship."

"Let her come forward."

From her seat in the space reserved for witnesses, a second woman advanced and stood beside the first. They exchanged looks which were like two blasts of flame.

Godiva Basset was a stocky woman with a determined jaw. Her blond hair, plaited in braids, and her gown, a long, plain kirtle of light blue with flowing sleeves, a good deal the worse for wear from her imprisonment, showed her to be of a somewhat higher class than a villein. Her accuser, Hawisa Turpin, was dressed in much the same fashion, but was tall and skinny, with a hooked nose and the wattled look of a vulture.

"Let me see the presentment in this case," remarked the presiding judge, and the clerk of the court, extracting a document from the pile of parchment rolls on his table, bustled up and handed it to him.

He scanned it, then passed it in turn to his two colleagues.

"Hawisa Turpin," he said then, "you have charged that in your absence the appellee, Godiva Basset, stole into your dwelling and there committed the crime of arson by setting it on fire, causing it to be consumed. What proof do you offer to support your charge?"

"Why, your Worship," Hawisa rasped, "there's no doubt on't at all. I'd been out a-marketing, and when I came back down the lane I saw Godiva Basset a-sneaking away from my house—"

"She lies!" cried Godiva. "I was nowhere near it, and—"

"Hold your tongue, baggage!" snapped the chief justice. "You will answer only when one of us speaks to you. Go on, Goodwife Turpin."

"Then I saw smoke a-coming from the thatch, and knew 'twas no fire on my hearth a-making such a great cloud. I ran to put it out, but the place was all afire in a trice. Burnt to a cinder, it did . . . and all *her* doing!"

She turned to Godiva. "Aye, thou didst this mischief, she-wolf! I'd fain pull that tow out of thy head and spin a rope to hang thee!"

Godiva forgot the judge's warning. "Try it!" she shrilled. "Try it, witch!"

And with that the women flew at each other, and went down in a heap, snarling, scratching, gouging at each other's eyes. Two bailiffs dived in and stood them on their feet. When order was restored, the chief justice threatened to have both whipped and then manacled if there was another outbreak. The two women then stood quietly, breathing hard, trembling, glaring at each other.

The presiding justice spoke to Godiva: "What say you to this evidence, Goodwife Basset?"

Godiva's voice shook. "She hates me, she does! That's why she's done this! Before God and Our Lady, your Worship, I never set fire to her house! I was nowhere near when it happened, and I can prove it by my neighbor, Goodwife Brewer, where I'd gone that day, and by others that saw me. Call them as witnesses, your Worship!"

The sheriff rose from his place and held up his hand for recognition. "If it please your Worships—"

"Yes, sheriff," said the chief justice.

"I see no reason to take up your time with the calling of

witnesses in this case. The appellant saw the appellee coming from her house just before it burst into flames. It is well known that Goodwife Basset has long been hostile toward Goodwife Turpin, and has made threats against her."

"Aye!" Hawisa burst out, "she made 'em! Said she'd sew my lips together and stop my lying!"

The presiding judge addressed Godiva: "Is this true, Goodwife Basset?"

For some moments the accused woman was silent. At last she nodded, and said in a voice that was hardly audible: "She's a scold, your Worship, that's always a-telling false tales of me! I wanted to stop her clacking tongue. But I never set her house afire!"

For a time the three judges put their heads together and consulted in whispers. Then the chief justice looked down once more at Godiva.

"Having heard the evidence in this case, our judgment is that it is of sufficient weight to justify our order that the sheriff of this county shall put you to his law, Goodwife Basset."

Godiva's shriek drowned out the excited buzz that rose from the spectators' section. She slumped and would have fallen to the floor if the bailiff standing near her had not leaped to her side and steadied her.

Then she cried out, "Nay! Nay! I know my rights! He can't put me to his law till twelve of my neighbors decide. They're here! Call them, your Worship! They'll tell you I didn't do it!"

She swung around, pointing an accusing finger straight at the sheriff. "He knows I'm innocent! When he came to take me he said he'd see I got proper justice if I didn't forget him, but I had no money! . . . Ask him what he got from Hawisa!"

"Be still!" admonished the chief justice. "We will hear no such ridiculous charges in this court."

He addressed the sheriff. "This prisoner is remanded to your custody. You will produce her at the lists at the hour of tierce tomorrow to undergo the ordeal by fire, thus to determine beyond all doubt her guilt or innocence of this charge."

At his words, Godiva collapsed in a faint, but when two bailiffs lifted her up she revived. Her wails and moans echoed through the courtroom as they bore her off to the dungeon.

All activity was at a standstill in the shire town the next morning. It seemed as if all its inhabitants, as well as those of the surrounding countryside for miles around, were jammed into the space surrounding the arena sixty feet square which had been laid out in a level field on the outskirts of the town. On one side, with its open front facing the arena, a tent had been erected for the itinerant justices. Flanking it were benches for the court attendants, while immediately in front another bench had been placed.

Within the arena, two flat stones had been set at a carefully measured distance of nine feet apart. At one of the corners of the lists stood a forge. Its charcoal fire pulsed and glowed with an angry glare as a smith plied its bellows.

A single peal from the bell of a church tower in the distance rang out, signifying the hour of tierce, nine o'clock. It had no sooner died away than a trumpeter sounded a blast and the scarlet-clad judges, followed by their train of attendants, appeared and marched solemnly to their places.

The sheriff strode to the forge and stood bent over it

while the smith poked into the glowing mass of charcoal with a rod. Then, nodding his head, the officer advanced before the judges.

"Is the iron ready?" asked the presiding judge.

"It is, your Worship."

"What is its weight?"

"It is of the middle weight of two pounds, your Worship."

"Very well," said the justice. "You may have the appellee and appellant fetched, sheriff."

The hum of voices among the spectators was instantly hushed. There was dead silence on the field as a bailiff led Godiva Basset, now manacled to prevent a possible escape, to her place in the lists before the judges' tent. Behind her, escorted by another bailiff, walked Hawisa Turpin.

Godiva's step was firm, and she held herself erect, but her face, so flushed with anger the preceding day, was chalk-white. She looked straight ahead, and seemed unconscious of the several thousand eyes fixed upon her. Her accuser, on the other hand, bore herself with an air of triumph, and her predatory eyes roved over the crowd as if to say, "I told you I'd fix her!"

The chief justice nodded to the clerk of the court, who rose from his bench, carrying a Bible. He placed the book in Godiva's right hand.

"Clasp Goodwife Turpin's right hand with thy left," he directed her.

When Godiva had done so, he continued: "Repeat this oath after me."

Those surrounding the lists could hear the clerk's voice clearly, but Godiva's, repeating his words, was little more than a whisper:

"Hear this, O woman whom I hold by the hand, who

calleth thyself Hawisa by name of baptism, that I who call
myself Godiva by name of baptism did not feloniously set
fire to thy house nor are in any way guilty in the said felony,
so help me God!"

Hawisa Turpin's voice was scornful when the clerk had
her swear a similar oath, again charging Godiva with arson.
Then, as the two women faced the judges, they swore in turn
a second oath:

"Hear this oath, justices. I have this day neither drunk
nor have I upon me bone, stone nor any enchantment, sor-
cery or witchcraft whereby the law of God may be abased
or the law of the Evil One exalted."

Ordinarily, when an ordeal by fire was held, a priest said
prayers, and the accused woman drank a cup of holy water
and sprinkled her hands with it. Since the interdict was still
in force, however, this ceremony was dispensed with.

A bailiff then led Godiva into the lists and removed her
chains. The silence now was awesome; it seemed that the
massed thousands were all holding their breath. Once, as
she walked up to the nearest of the stone markers, the accused woman faltered, but quickly recovered herself.

The bailiff placed her with her left foot touching the
marker, and explained how she might stretch out her right
foot as far as possible toward the second one. In this her tall,
long-legged accuser would have been better off, for Godiva's
short legs could not stretch as far.

"Thou must keep the iron in thy hands till thou reach the
second stone," the bailiff cautioned her. "Drop it and thou'lt
stand convicted."

All was now ready. At a signal from the sheriff, the smith
reached into his fire with a pair of tongs and drew forth the
heated bar of iron. It glowed a dull red like some immense,

malevolent eye. Brilliant sparks of slag and fuel, like tiny shooting stars, flew sizzling from it. The short, chunky smith bore the iron toward Godiva. In that moment a kind of great sigh like a soughing wind escaped the spectators.

For the barest instant, Godiva's eyes rested in horror upon the iron, and she shrank away from it. Then she seized it in her hands.

It was over in a flash of time. Some of the spectators felt cheated, as though they had seen nothing of the frightful spectacle they had come to witness. They heard a piercing scream, and saw a figure hurtle toward the second marker like a boulder propelled by a catapult. Then Godiva lay motionless on the ground, as if she were a heap of rags. The iron fell to the earth, bounded crazily once or twice, then came to rest. A cloud of blue smoke swirled up; then the dry grass where it lay burst into a small flame.

The bailiff, who had been stationed to watch, raised his arms over his head and nodded toward the judges' tent to signify that Godiva's foot had touched the second marker before she collapsed and dropped the iron. Other attendants rushed to the unconscious woman's side. Using great care, they wrapped her hands in linen and bound the bandages so they could not be removed. Then they carried her away from the lists.

Godiva was not to know her fate at once. For three days she languished in the dungeon beneath the shire hall, and was fed the scanty prisoners' fare by her jailer, for she could not hold the spoon. Then, on the third morning, she was brought before the justices in the courtroom once more.

As yet no one could tell the condition of her swathed hands, but there was no doubt in the minds of those in the

packed chamber as to what she had endured. Her eyes were
sunken in a face as gaunt as that of her accuser, and she
cowered before the judges like some frightened animal which
has been beaten.

At a sign from the chief justice, Godiva's bandages were
unbound and unrolled, and she advanced to the dais that
the three men might inspect her hands. The spectators heard
them gasp, and all shook their heads in wonderment. It was
not the first time they had looked at the hands of a woman
after an ordeal by fire, but never had they seen a pair like
these after the allotted three days.

"There is no sign that the hands of the appellant Godiva
Basset have been burned." Regret seemed to tinge the chief
justice's voice. "She is accordingly declared innocent of
felony and is discharged."

There were some in the courtroom who muttered that in
spite of Godiva's oath, there had been witchcraft afoot that
day in the lists, and the most vehement among them was
Hawisa Turpin before she flounced from the chamber.
Others piously crossed themselves and ascribed her deliver-
ance to a miracle sent by God. Whatever the truth, Godiva
Basset, illegally put to the sheriff's "law" by the unscrupulous
servants of an unscrupulous king without the judgment of
her neighbors, had escaped the further consequences of failure in her ordeal by fire.

Ordeals were not among the wrongs originated by King
John, for they went back far before his time, but he and some
of his unprincipled officers used them for their own gain.

An innocent man might find himself charged by an enemy
with a murder he did not commit, and brought before the
King's justices. Henry II had wisely given such persons pro-

A Wagon Load of Soldiers

Trial By Battle

Monk Illuminating

A Dishonest Baker's Punishment

Scenes from 13th Century English Life

tection under the law. They could plead that the accusation was made out of hate and spite, and obtain a document called a writ of inquisition of life or limb.

The writ allowed the accused person to have twelve neighbors testify in his behalf. But under John's rule he had to pay for the document. If the evidence against the accused was strong enough, he could be put to a sheriff's "law" and subjected to an ordeal. But often enough in John's reign his justices and sheriffs ignored this law, especially if they were paid by an accused person's enemies to do so.

A writ of inquisition of life or limb could save an innocent man's life. Lacking it, he could be put to the ordeal of trial by combat without the evidence of his neighbors to help him clear himself. The only exceptions were cases in which there could be no question of the man's guilt; he was then hanged immediately.

In trial by combat, the accused and his accuser fought all day to decide the case. Although they wore some armor, carried shields and fought with batons tipped with horn, which were less deadly than swords or broadaxes, one of the combatants was sometimes killed. And if the accused man yielded by crying, "Craven!" he was adjudged guilty and hanged. Trial by combat was even used to decide suits brought in disputes over ownership of land.

Other ordeals were those of fire, used chiefly for women accused of felonies, and trial by water, in which the defendant was thrown into a pond or river. If he floated or swam he was guilty; if he sank and drowned, his family at least had the satisfaction of knowing he had died an innocent man.

In general, ordeals fell more heavily upon the common people than the nobility; thus the abuse of justice in such cases was not among the barons' chief grievances. But in

Paris, Stephen Langton was not ignorant of what was going on in England.

The cause of the common people was nearer Langton's heart than that of the barons. Whether a woman like Godiva Basset was guilty or not, she was wronged when she was not given a just trial under the law. When the time came for drawing up Magna Carta, the cardinal would not forget such miscarriages of justice.

6

In the summer of 1211, King John and his army rampaged into Wales and put down the revolt there as quickly and decisively as had been done in Ireland. To ensure that the Welsh chieftains would cause him no more trouble, John seized twenty-eight of their sons as hostages.

On his way back to London, he stopped at the shire town of Northampton and issued a decree levying a scutage upon all his English barons who had failed to march into Wales with him.

Scutage was one form of an ancient feudal tax by which a nobleman could be excused from doing military service in return for paying the king a sum of money. The amount varied according to the extent of the lands the baron held. It had long been in effect, but while Henry II had been satisfied with a moderate scutage, Richard had increased it, and John had then doubled his brother's levy, an action which

73

the barons bitterly resented. It was one more link in the chain of grievances being forged against King John.

John's stop at Northampton was not merely to levy the scutage, however, but for a far more important purpose, and one which held dire consequences for the future. Pope Innocent had sent two new envoys to negotiate with him—a cardinal named Pandulf, and Durand, a member of the powerful order of the Knights Templar. Finding the King absent from London, they had proceeded to Northampton to meet him.

The conference was held in John's castle there. The King, triumphant after his quick victory in Wales, was in an arrogant mood, and wasted no time on the polite phrases of diplomacy.

"You may tell your master in Rome that if his creature Langton, the false claimant to the see of Canterbury, dares set foot in England we will hang him!" he flared when the emissaries had explained their mission.

Pandulf was a suave and adroit diplomat, but the King's belligerence angered him. "His Holiness is a reasonable man," he said severely, "but we are instructed to inform you that unless you are also reasonable he is prepared to take further steps to assure your obedience to the laws of God and Holy Church."

"Let him!" John roared. "Has he not yet learned he cannot dictate to the King of England?"

Durand then spoke: "If you are unwilling to negotiate with us, Sire, we must inform you that unless you allow Stephen Cardinal Langton to assume his chair of Canterbury, we are instructed to publish to you his Apostolic Highness' pronouncement of excommunication for maliciously depriving the Church of its rights. As you know, it was issued two years ago, but its publication in England was held in abeyance in the hope that a settlement of this matter might be reached."

"Ha!" the King raged, "does your master think by this to bring us to terms? If it is no more successful than the interdict, we welcome it!"

"The Holy Father is not without other means of defending the Church against its enemies." Pandulf eyed the King narrowly. "I warn you to remember, Sire, that your subjects, while bound to you by their oaths of loyalty, made before God, have a higher duty of obedience to Him through the laws of Holy Church. . . ."

John's jaw sagged. Was this a threat? Suppose the Pope released all English subjects from their oaths of obedience to the Crown. It might encourage the treasonable barons to strike. He felt cold beads of sweat on his brow.

"We did not mean that we refuse to receive Langton under any circumstances," he said in a milder tone. "Let him come to England, after first resigning his chair of Canterbury, and we will find another see for him."

"I regret that your proposal will not be acceptable to his Holiness," Pandulf replied quickly.

John fell silent, the enraged flush on his face turning to a pallor when Pandulf made his veiled threat. The two envoys knew only too well how much he would like to take some frightful revenge upon them.

"Very well," said the King at last, "we will receive Langton as Archbishop of Canterbury, provided our right to select future archbishops is recognized by the Pope."

The two men saw through the subterfuge at once. In one

way or another, John would waste no time in getting rid of
Stephen Langton and appointing a man of his own choice as
soon as Langton assumed his duties.

Pandulf shook his head. "I regret that I cannot speak for
his Apostolic Highness, but nevertheless I am certain that
he will never consent to give up the rights of the Church."

"Nor will we give up ours!" stormed the King.

"Then I must inform you that the Holy Father's pronouncement of excommunication upon you is now in full
effect," said Pandulf. And the two envoys rose, bowed and
took their departure for Rome.

John's excommunication soon had tragic consequences, not
for himself, however, but for a poor royal clerk in his Exchequer.

The Exchequer, which handled the finances of the kingdom, occupied a kind of turret attached to Westminster Hall
on the side facing the river Thames. It was stuck on there as
though at the last minute the architect had tried to make the
hall presentable, for the turret was more ornamental than
the rest of the barren-looking building, and its top was a
notched battlement like that of a castle tower.

Inside this turret one morning, following the King's return to London, a group of royal clerks were sitting about a
table in a room just off the larger chamber which was the
Court of the Exchequer. They were clergymen—priests,
monks and one or two of higher degree—in long robes of
black or gray, encircled at the waist by girdles, and all having
shaven bare spots on top of their heads.

If they had looked out of the room's single window with
its arched top, they would have seen the busy panorama of
the river, craft of all kinds, from wherries to good-sized
ships, moving up and down. But their eyes were fastened

upon the clutter of parchment documents before them on the table. One or two were busily scratching away with quill pens.

All activity ceased, however, as a man entered the little room, William of Ely, King John's Treasurer of the Exchequer.

"Is all in order?" Ely seemed fidgety, and his voice had a nervous edge.

"Everything is ready, my Lord Treasurer," said one of the clerks.

"You have the pipe rolls from the last session at hand?"

"Aye, my Lord, and those from the one before as well."

"Make sure nothing is missing. The King will be present at the session today." Ely's eyes swept over the group of clerks. "Geoffrey, you will handle the calculations. You had better go in at once, so that his Majesty will not be kept waiting when he appears. The chancellor and the sheriffs have already arrived."

Geoffrey, an archdeacon, gathered up a great bundle of parchment rolls from the table and followed William of Ely out. He was a slight, mild-looking man with a scholar's pale face. In the Exchequer chamber he took his place at a table adjoining a much larger and longer one in the center of the room. On the smaller table was a heap of round wooden counters, and for some moments Geoffrey busied himself stacking them in neat piles. Then he looked about at a scene which was familiar to him from long experience.

The treasurer had seated himself along one side of the great table, which was also occupied by Walter de Grey, the King's chancellor, Richard Marsh, senior clerk of the Chancery, and several other officials of the Chancery and Exchequer. One chair, in the center, was left vacant.

On the opposite side of the table sat eight hard-faced, bold-eyed men, all noblemen, arrayed in long, wide-sleeved tunics and mantles of bright colors. Geoffrey knew them all, for he had often seen them there before. They were sheriffs, whose duties included collecting the King's revenues, and whose accounts were to be audited that day.

Just then the door connecting the Court of the Exchequer with the main hall was thrown open. Those in the room rose and knelt as King John, followed by several of his attendants, came in.

He laid aside his mantle and stood for a moment surveying the scene, an imperious figure in his long tunic of white samite embroidered with golden fleurs-de-lis, its enormous sleeves drooping almost to his knees. The scowl on his face deepened as he gazed at the eight sheriffs. Then he moved to the vacant chair, seated himself and made a sign to the rest, who rose and resumed their places.

The King spoke to William of Ely: "Proceed with the audits."

The treasurer nodded to Geoffrey, who took up a parchment roll from those before him and began to read: "Revenues collected by Roger de Hayton, sheriff, two hundred, twoscore and four pounds, eight shillings, sixpence."

From the stacks on his table, Geoffrey took twenty-two counters. In the center of the larger table was a black cloth divided by white lines into squares like those of a checkerboard. Across the top row he distributed the counters in five of the squares.

As a scholar, Geoffrey needed no such arrangement to show him the revenues Sheriff Hayton had collected from the shire or county of which he was the King's chief officer. The clerk could write the amount on parchment, but many

of the sheriffs could neither read nor write, much less per-
form calculations in Roman numerals. By looking at the
counters, however—two in the square whose column stood
for hundreds, two in the next one for scores, four in that
for pounds, then eight in the one for shillings and six in
the last for pence—Hayton could see that the amount of
money he had collected was shown properly.

Geoffrey began to read again from the parchment: "Expenses. . . ."

"Hold!" Startled at the interruption, he looked up to find
the King's piercing gaze fastened upon him. "What were the
revenues shown on the pipe rolls for our sheriff, Hayton, at
the corresponding session last year?"

The clerk shuffled through the parchments on his table,
drew out one of them, unrolled and scanned it. "The amount,
Sire, was three hundred, fourscore and five pounds, four
shillings, ninepence."

Looking up, Geoffrey saw anger in the King's eyes. John
was speaking to the sheriff: "Your collections for this session
are far short of those of last year. How is this?"

"The harvest was poor this year, Sire . . . the drought.
. . ."

The King turned to the treasurer. "What of the others
whose accounts have already been audited? Have they fallen
short?"

"In general they are about the same as last year's collections, my liege."

"Ha!" cried the King, "how much money have you held
back from the accounting, Hayton?"

There was anger in the sheriff's eyes, too, but it was mixed
with fear. "I have held nothing back, Sire!"

Geoffrey had seen these mounting rages before at times

when the King chose to preside in person over the audits of his revenues. He knew the signs.

"A lie!" The King fairly screamed the words at the sheriff. Then he called out: "Agelric! Arrest this knave and put him in Purgatory for safekeeping until an inquest into his accounts can be held. We will see what he has done with the Crown's money!"

A soldier in ring mail, carrying a spear and standing guard at the door of the chamber, threw it open and summoned two others, who tramped in and seized the unfortunate sheriff, each by an arm. Geoffrey did not miss the look of black hatred which Hayton darted at John as he was led away.

The King's eyes rested menacingly on the other sheriffs. "Let all who are against us take heed! We will find you out in your knaveries"—he seized a counter from the checkered cloth, gripped it with his teeth, tore it in two and spat the pieces on the table—"and crush you!"

Geoffrey felt the flesh crawl on the back of his neck as he replaced the counter. Such outbursts never failed to make him uneasy at the power of this king whose terrible wrath could fall without warning upon anyone he suspected of fraud or against whom he held a grudge. Hayton, Geoffrey knew, might remain for weeks in "Purgatory," the dungeon under Westminster Hall where political and other prisoners were held until they could be investigated or brought to trial.

The King seemed calmer when the accounts of the next man had been audited, and his collections found to be slightly above those for the previous year's session of the Court. He sharply questioned one or two sheriffs whose returns did not fully satisfy him, but the morning drew to a close without further displays of temper. When the session adjourned for dinner, Geoffrey went into the room where his fellow clerks were still laboring with their pens.

He heaved a sigh and lowered his voice: "A bad time in there this morning. He's in a frightful humor." He told his colleagues what had happened, and added, "I don't believe my Lord Hayton stole any money."

"Perhaps not," said one of the others, "but he might have kept out of trouble. All he had to do was to hold court oftener and fine the peasants who could not take the time to attend as the law requires of them. That's what the smart ones do. And increase the fines against those convicted of offenses. They have to produce the money or go to jail, you know. Then Hayton would have had more to show in there."

"My Lord Hayton scorns such injustice," said Geoffrey. "He is a righteous man. Besides, why should anyone be seized and cast into prison without some evidence of his wrongdoing?"

A canon said, "There is nothing any of us can do about it, Geoffrey. Why concern yourself? After all, it is not as if this were the only injustice in England."

"There'll be more of it, mark you," said a monk, "especially against those of the Church. No wonder the King is in an ugly mood today. He has had bad news from Rome."

"What is that?" Geoffrey asked.

"The Pope's envoys published the sentence of excommunication upon him at Northampton. I heard of it from the abbot this morning."

"Excommunicated!" Geoffrey was aghast. "What are we going to do?"

The monk shrugged. "Wait for orders from our superiors, I suppose. We may have to flee from England, but I doubt it. When the Holy Father placed the interdict upon England, the King swore he would gouge out the eyes and slit the nostrils of every clerk he could lay his hands on. But, you see, it did not happen. What would he do without us to keep the records of his revenues?"

Geoffrey shook his head. "This is different, Robert. The laws of the Church forbid us to have anything to do with excommunicated persons. I was sorely disturbed when the news came that the excommunication had been published in France, although the abbot counseled us that since it had not been published in England it was not effective here. But now we can serve the King no longer."

"Calm yourself, Geoffrey," said one of the others. "Marry, there is no need for haste. Pope Innocent, I understand, has ordered the excommunication published throughout the kingdom, but what bishop or archbishop dares do so? I say that if all in England are not made aware of the decree, it is not in effect, and we need not worry."

"But it is true that the Holy Father's envoys relayed it to the King, is it not?"

"There can be no doubt of that," said the monk who had first spoken of it.

Geoffrey was silent, and for a time the only sound in the room was the scratching of pens. But at last he said, "It is our duty to leave this place and serve the King no longer. I shall do so at once."

"Are you mad?" demanded one of his colleagues. "A royal servant must have the King's permission to leave. Do you think for a moment that he will grant it? Why, he will crush you as you told us he did with the counter."

"I shall not seek the King's permission. I am obeying the order of the Holy Father."

"You are a lack-brain!" cried another.

Geoffrey rose. "Will you not join me, my brothers, in leaving the service of this man who has sinned against the Church?"

He saw only terror in their faces, however. Without another word he left the chamber and made his way to the palace yard, in which many of the clerks had secured houses from the abbot in order to be near the Exchequer. In the one he occupied he threw himself upon his knees in prayer, and then gave himself up to silent contemplation. Wholly dedicated to the Church, Geoffrey was convinced he had done the only thing possible under the decree of excommunication.

He did not long continue his meditation, however, for he was well aware what the consequences of his act would be once his absence from the Exchequer was discovered. He rose from his knees, hurriedly gathered together in a bundle such of his belongings as he would need on a journey, and set out on one of the roads leading away from London.

Geoffrey must also have known how small were his chances of escaping King John's terrible vengeance. As to where his flight took him, and exactly what happened when he was overtaken and captured, the historians of that long-ago time do not agree. One account says he was taken near Dunstaple; another that he reached Nottingham. Probably he hoped to find refuge in some abbey or convent where he had friends.

The accounts of his fate differ too. One says that he was tortured to death in Nottingham Castle; a second that he was imprisoned and died a lingering death in Bristol Castle. The most frightful of the stories has it that because Geoffrey was of the Church, King John had him encased in a sheet of lead shaped like a cope, a cloaklike vestment worn by Roman

Catholic clergymen at certain ceremonies, and left to starve. All are agreed that he was imprisoned and perished, probably in a horrible manner.

Neither Hayton nor Geoffrey had committed a serious crime. Geoffrey had merely disobeyed the custom which required him as a servant of the King to obtain permission before leaving his post. Yet he was seized and thrown into a dungeon without trial—to die.

He was only one of many men of the nobility and common people, as well as the clergy, who were imprisoned or suffered other harsh penalties without being tried for what they were accused of doing. This was one of the greatest wrongs which Magna Carta sought to correct, and the chapter which forbids the king to seize, imprison, exile or destroy a man, or to take his property without giving him a fair trial, is one of the most important of the Great Charter's provisions.

John stirred anger, hatred and a rebellious impulse among the nobility by persecution of his enemies, like that of his revenge upon the Briouses, his decrees of outlawry and seizure of barons' properties, his holding of their sons as hostages to insure their fathers' obedience and good behavior, and his levies of crushing taxes and exorbitant fines. His quarrel with the Church, seizure of its properties, and such retaliations as that against the clerk Geoffrey, turned the clergy against him. The taxes and fines also fell upon the lower orders, as did the ignoring of accused persons' rights to a fair trial, and the command that hedges around tilled land within royal forest boundaries be burned and ditches leveled. In time the common people, too, came to hate the King.

So far, however, uprisings against him had taken place only among the unruly chieftains of Wales and Ireland. But in 1212 something more serious than whispers of resentment was stirring among the English barons, particularly the turbulent lords of the northern shires. At secret meetings in their castles amid the wild moors and hills, indignant mutterings turned to demands for action. And now these rebellious spirits had two leaders who were among the King's bitterest and most vengeful enemies.

7

In the Northumberland stronghold of Alnwick, a dozen barons lounged about the high table in the great hall of the castle's keep. The place was murky with smoke, for although it was early summer, the east wind off the North Sea blew damp and chill over the moorlands, and the warmth of the fire on the hearth was gratefully welcomed.

The ladies had withdrawn to a smaller chamber off the main hall. The barons, relaxing after the day's hunt, stuffed with venison, their wits dulled by the spiced wine they had drunk, were only now beginning to revive as they regaled themselves with drafts of ale.

Eustace de Vesci, lord of the castle, rose from his seat.

"Hold!" he cried. "Enough of your plaints. They get us nowhere. FitzWalter, our worthy comrade from the South, has journeyed here to tell us what he knows of affairs in London. Let him speak!"

As Robert FitzWalter rose, Vesci beckoned to his master butler and whispered in his ear. Butler and cupbearers then withdrew from the hall.

FitzWalter was cast in a somewhat smoother mold than those who now gave him their close attention, yet for all their ferocious and ruffianly appearance, the men of the North could not match the rapacity of this lord of Benington Castle in Hertfordshire. FitzWalter and his close ally, Eustace de Vesci, both bitter enemies of the King, were unprincipled rogues, as grasping and ambitious for power as John himself.

"The King prepares to return to France," FitzWalter told them. "If he be not thwarted, he may well regain the lands he lost there, and so strengthen his power, which heaven forfend! If a blow is to be struck, it must be soon."

"Softly, softly, Robert, lest perchance you be overheard," cautioned Vesci. "I doubt not that all of us here are to be trusted." He shot a glance over the company that seemed dubious in spite of the smile on his face. "But remember, the ears of Judases clog keyholes and ride the very flames that lick up on yonder hearth."

FitzWalter, too, let his eyes swing over the circle of his hearers, probing each in turn—Robert de Vaux of Cumberland; Richard de Umfraville, lord of Prudhoe Castle in Northumberland; David, Earl of Huntingdon; Richard de Lucy of Egremont; Robert de Ros, baron of the Northumberland castle of Wark; and the rest. He seemed to be trying to measure not only their trustworthiness, but the support each could furnish in knights, soldiers and money. Most of them, he knew, held deep-seated grudges against the King for one reason or another.

Then, lowering his voice, he asked, "What say you? Do we join and strike?"

"Yea, faith, I'll join!" cried Lucy.

FitzWalter nodded. He had known Lucy was one who could be counted upon, for the lord of the barony of Copeland had not forgotten the exorbitant fine John had wrung from him in return for clearing him of charges that he had improperly carried out his duties as royal forester of Cumberland.

Richard de Umfraville did not agree so quickly, however. "For my part," he said, "that is as it may be, my Lord Robert. Tell us, what support is to come from the barons of the South?"

"A goodly host will stand ready," FitzWalter replied. "There's Earl Richard de Clare of Hertford—"

"Aye," cut in Vesci, "he'll be with us, athirst for revenge upon the tyrant for the murder of his daughter's husband, young William de Briouse, Henry de Bohun, Earl of Hereford, as well, being also a kinsman of the Briouses."

"William de Mowbray has not forgotten how the King tricked him into paying two thousand marks for justice in his suit over land against William de Stutville, and then decided the case against him," FitzWalter went on. And he mentioned others who were certain to join the plot.

"What is the plan?" the Earl of Huntingdon asked.

"Perchance fortune may play into our hands," replied FitzWalter. "It is rumored in London that the Welsh chieftains, their wounds now healed, are restive once more and preparing to rise against the King. This may cause him to forbear his invasion of France for the time, and march against Wales. In such case, we could strike in his rear while he is engaged with the Welshmen. Meanwhile, we shall seize his family, making sure the line of succession no longer threatens the kingdom. . . ."

FitzWalter's dark smile left no doubt in the minds of the

barons as to the fate intended for John's children—Henry, the heir apparent, Richard, his second son, and his daughter, the Princess Joan.

"His palace of Westminster must be taken, since the Exchequer and Treasury are there," FitzWalter continued, "as well as his fortified castles. The Londoners chafe under the King's oppression, and the city will fall to us. Then, with the royal army trapped between ours and the Welsh . . ." His outspread hands were a gesture of finality.

There was more discussion, more questions were asked, and at length a general agreement was reached on the plan for treason.

De Vesci then spoke: "We will hold ourselves in readiness while my Lord Robert returns south. Upon a signal from him, we will march." He held up a warning hand. "Take heed, all of you—not a whisper of this must reach those who would betray us!"

Surveying them, he wondered uneasily again whether there might be a traitor among them . . . Ros? The lord of Wark had married one of William the Lion's daughters . . . and William was now on better terms with John. Yet on reflection, Vesci saw that it was as unjust to suspect Ros as to question his own motives on that score, for he, too, had married a daughter of the Scottish King.

FitzWalter rode south the next morning. His prediction of a revolt in Wales soon proved correct, and King John, abandoning his plan to invade France, hastily summoned his army to assemble at Chester, on the Welsh border. Then he set out for that town with his household, which included the twenty-eight young Welsh knights he had taken as hostages.

As he rode through forest and meadow at the head of the cavalcade, the King could not help but notice the lack of enthusiasm among the people when he traversed towns and villages. His officers seized what food and supplies were needed along the way, since feudal custom permitted the King this privilege, known as purveyance, provided they were paid for at the market price. Those who had to yield these things up gave John's men stony looks, however. The tallies issued by the Exchequer which were given as payment —sticks of wood notched to show their value—were good only to pay taxes and other Crown revenues.

Even when payment in money was made in such cases, it was often months before it was received. And the King's officers paid only what they pleased, not the regular price.

There was hatred in the glances turned upon the procession by lords and ladies of some manors they passed. Too many had been forced to surrender their sons as hostages to the suspicious King, and many of their daughters had been sold in marriage. Feudal law required the King's permission before women of his vassals' families could marry. John took advantage of it by selling young women, and also the widows of barons, to the highest bidder.

Occasionally some spirited lady thwarted him. When his baron, Ralph of Cornhill, died, the King decided that his attractive widow should marry a French nobleman of his household, Godfrey of Louvain. Since she detested Godfrey, she desperately gathered together what money she could raise and offered it to John. It amounted to only four hundred pounds, and although she added three fine saddle horses and two hawks, Godfrey had offered eight hundred pounds! There was no recourse, but when the Frenchman came for his bride, she had fled from the kingdom.

This practice of John's of bringing noblemen from France to become members of the royal household was bitterly resented by the barons. They felt they were being robbed of what should have been theirs when the King appointed his foreign favorites as sheriffs and to other high posts.

While John was on the road, several figures loomed up ahead. When the cavalcade came up with them they proved to be sheriff's officers dragging a man along with them.

"What have we here?" asked the King.

"This dog held up a priest on the road and robbed and murdered him, my liege," said one of the officers. "What shall we do with him?"

John's laugh revealed all his intense hatred of the clergy. "Let the fellow go," he said. "He has only gotten rid of one of our enemies."

One of the most fiendish of all his cruelties was soon to come. At Nottingham he heard an alarming piece of news. De Vesci's fears that word of the northern barons' treasonable plans might be spread abroad were all too well founded. Somehow the plot had reached William the Lion's ears. A messenger arrived with a warning from the Scottish monarch.

At the same time, John heard other rumors even more disturbing. The barons' uprising was said to be already under way, his second son Richard had been killed, his young queen brutally attacked by the insurgents, and a royal treasury at Gloucester looted.

These latter reports were to prove false, but John instantly decided to turn his army about and abandon the expedition.

"Since we cannot teach these treasonable Welsh chieftains another lesson ourself," he said, "we will do it in another way. Let their twenty-eight sons we hold as hostages be hanged immediately."

And with the young men's bodies swinging from the gallows trees, he made plans to strike at his rebellious barons.

The reports contained the names of the two leaders in the conspiracy—Robert FitzWalter and Eustace de Vesci. De Vesci was safe enough in his castle of Alnwick in the craggy northern moorlands, only a short distance from the even wilder mountains across the border in Scotland. But Robert FitzWalter held castles within striking distance.

"Blow the trumpets!" John ordered. "March for Fitz-Walter's castle of Benington in Hertfordshire, and then to London and his Baynard Castle. Both places are to be destroyed."

The destruction was carried out, but FitzWalter escaped to France. Eustace de Vesci, hearing that the plot had been discovered, fled to Scotland.

Nevertheless, events were moving slowly but surely toward a crisis. Although the King displayed no sign of worry over his excommunication to those about him, inwardly he raged and fretted. He had nipped the plot against him, and declared FitzWalter and Vesci outlaws so they would not dare return to England. But who else was involved?

John cared not a whit that he had been expelled from the Church and damned. But the threat uttered by Pandulf persisted in tormenting him. Could it be that his barons had been secretly released from their oaths of allegiance by the Pope, and that the pontiff was urging them to revolt? . . .

He called together those of his advisers whom he trusted as far as he ever trusted anyone.

"Who else among our barons was involved in the plot against us?" he demanded.

"It is the northern barons who are the most unruly, Sire," one suggested. "Perhaps Richard de Umfraville. . . ."

"Send a demand that he surrender his castle of Prudhoe and his four sons as hostages," John ordered.

"The Earl of Huntingdon may be involved," was another comment. "He has not forgotten how his father's castles were destroyed by your father after the revolt of 1173."

"Send Hugh de Neville with a force to seize his castle of Fotheringay and his son as hostage."

John applied the same treatment to others he suspected, but he had no feeling of security. Soon afterward he heard something which, though he took no stock in it, did not help his peace of mind. A hermit named Peter of Pontefract had made an ominous prediction. Hermits were thought to have the power of foretelling the future, and also to heal diseases. People often came to the forest huts or caves in which they lived to seek advice or a cure for their ills. From his retreat in Yorkshire, Peter had preached to such a group.

"The King will not reign more than fourteen years," he declared. "He will not be king on next Ascension Day, and his crown will pass to another." In no time his words spread all over England and were widely believed.

While John was not as credulous as the ignorant peasants of England, he nevertheless hesitated to destroy Peter lest it turn more of his subjects against him. He sent men to Yorkshire who seized and dragged the hermit before him.

In high dudgeon, John demanded, "What are these lies you have told of us, mongrel?"

The tattered recluse with his tangled and matted hair and beard looked the King steadfastly in the eye.

"Rest assured that on the aforesaid day you will not be a king," he insisted, "and if I am proved to have told a lie, do what you will with me."

"Put this refuge for fleas in chains and throw him into a dungeon in our castle of Corfe!" John bawled to his seneschal. "Let him remain there till Ascension Day, and when his parcel of lies is proved false we will deal with him as he deserves!"

The next Ascension Day would fall on May 16, 1213. John had been crowned on May 27, 1199; thus if Peter of Pontefract's prediction came true, his reign would have lasted a few days less than fourteen years.

The fact that John sent Peter to massive Corfe Castle in Dorsetshire near the Channel coast, which he considered the strongest fortress in his realm, shows that he wanted the hermit kept where he could not escape and do more mischief with his tongue.

Whether Pope Innocent learned of Peter's prediction or not, he took steps that could have made it come true if they had succeeded. In the fall of 1212, Stephen Langton and the refugee Bishops of London and Ely were summoned to Rome. Innocent asked them what effect John's excommunication had had upon England.

"It is more than four years since your Holiness placed the interdict upon England," Langton replied. "Both it and the excommunication have failed."

"Then this apostate must be deposed from his throne," said the pontiff. He turned to Pandulf, who was present at the audience. "Go with our Archbishop of Canterbury and our Bishops of London and Ely to Paris. Tell Philip Augustus of France that we desire him to carry out our command."

The French king was delighted to receive papal authority to invade England. Having beaten John once and taken away his domains in France, he now had visions of himself as King of both France and England. He began to assemble an army and a fleet for an invasion.

In John he had a formidable foe, however. As soon as the English king heard what was going on in France, he gathered together a tremendous army. And now the barons gave him full support, not because they loved him, but because their own lands were threatened by a French invasion.

The immense army from all over England mustered at Barham Down, near Canterbury and not far from the Channel coast. It was so vast that immediately there was trouble in feeding the soldiers. Even what John's officers, armed with the right of purveyance, could seize in the way of provisions was not enough.

John then sent all the inexperienced men home. He could afford to, for even then he still had sixty thousand veterans to repel the French invasion.

Meanwhile, the wily Pandulf, thinking that John might be intimidated by Philip Augustus' preparations, decided to have one more try at conciliation. He sent two Knights Templar across the Channel to Dover. John met them there.

The King was no more ready to agree to the Pope's demands than before, but the specter of Pandulf's threat that all English subjects might be released from their oaths of allegiance still haunted him. If he could make a settlement on his own terms . . .

"Go back to France," he told the envoys, "and return here with Pandulf."

They did so. The parley was held on May 13, 1213, in the great fortress of Dover Castle, perched high above the sea on the chalk cliffs of England.

"I repeat what I said during our last interview, your Majesty," Pandulf began, "that while his Holiness is a reasonable man, you will do well to be reasonable too. The King of France has a great army ready to overwhelm all England."

John's eyes flashed. "Let him come!"

"He has a vast fleet. . . ."

"Ours will sink it!" The King was perfectly confident, knowing his navy was superior in fighting qualities. He was counting on it to destroy the French fleet before the invaders ever reached shore.

"Then," said Pandulf, "perhaps it will interest you that the King of France has letters from most of your barons offering their support when he reaches England."

The effect these words produced upon John was as if a projectile from a catapult had crashed into the conference chamber. He gave a great start and turned deathly pale. What Pandulf had said was probably not true, though Philip Augustus may have made such a boast to the papal envoy. But John, tormented by his suspicions, was all too ready to believe it.

The barons had deceived him, he thought, by coming to his aid; when the French army began its invasion they would betray him. There flashed into his mind a vision of his fleet's commander, his close kinsman, William Plantagenet, Earl of Salisbury. John had treated him well, yet William was an ambitious man. The King's darting suspicions pricked him again as he recalled that William had favored pardons for the outlaw Fulk FitzWarin and his band. Was he, too, among the plotters, prepared to let the French fleet reach England unmolested?

John bowed his head. "It pleases us to accept your master's terms," he muttered.

The exultant Pandulf could hardly believe he had heard aright. As he began to name the conditions under which the Pope would lift the interdict and excommunication, he was prepared to find the King seeking to dodge, evade and bargain.

"Are you willing, Sire, to abide by the commands of his

Apostolic Highness in all matters for which his excommunication was placed upon you?" the envoy asked.

"We will do so," said John.

"Are you prepared to allow Stephen Cardinal Langton to come to England and assume his chair of Canterbury? And to guarantee his safety and that of the exiled Bishops of London, Ely, Hereford, Bath and Lancaster, as well as the prior and monks of Canterbury, and all other clergymen who have fled from your kingdom?"

"They shall return in full safety."

"You will promise they shall not be hindered in the performance of their duties?"

Again John nodded.

"There are certain other exiles, not of the clergy, who have sought the protection of the Church, Sire." Pandulf glanced at the King, and ignored the storm signals. "Will you revoke your decree of outlawry against Robert FitzWalter and Eustace de Vesci?"

This, of all that Pandulf had so far demanded, was the most difficult for John to swallow. FitzWalter and Vesci were archtraitors, but by posing as martyrs they had gained the support of the Church.

The King, in his panic, agreed, however. Pandulf then struck at the point which John's greed had made a stumbling block in all the previous negotiations: "Will you restore all Church property which you seized after the interdict was laid upon England?"

For the first time John's avarice forced an objection from him: "There are the customary and lawful dues the Church has always paid to the Crown upon its properties. . . ."

"It is not the desire of the Holy Father to take from you any revenues which would have been paid had there been no interdict," Pandulf asserted. "However, revenues which have been lost to the Church during the interdict must be returned. As a token of your good faith, the sum of eight thousand pounds must be delivered to me at once in part payment."

Even this demand the panic-stricken king accepted. Yet before signing an agreement he must make sure his own interests were protected. "We must have your assurance in writing and upon oath," he said, "that the clergy will make no attempt upon us or our crown."

"It shall be done," Pandulf promised.

And with that, clerks were summoned to draw up the peace charter. It was quickly prepared, and in the presence of Pandulf's retinue and John's advisers the King affixed his royal seal to the document.

He was still not satisfied, however. What would Philip Augustus do when he learned that the vast sums of money he had spent in preparation for the invasion had been thrown away? Might he not come anyway? And what would the treasonable barons do if he did?

John thought he had an answer to the problem. Two days later, on May 15, a great spectacle took place on the plain outside Dover Castle. The royal army in full battle array was drawn up there as a vast multitude of people from the surrounding countryside watched. In their presence, John handed a document to Pandulf.

"Having gravely offended God and Holy Mother Church in many ways," he said, "we are unworthy of divine mercy. Therefore, by this charter, attested by the barons of our Council, the Archbishop of Dublin and the Bishop of Norwich, we surrender our realms of England and Ireland to

God and the apostles Peter and Paul in the person of his Holiness, Pope Innocent III."

Then, removing his golden crown and handing it to Pandulf, he knelt and swore: "We, John, by the grace of God King of England and Lord of Ireland, will from this time forth be faithful to our liege lord, Pope Innocent, and his Catholic successors."

As John rose, Pandulf put the crown back on his head and restored his kingdom to him as a vassal of the Pope.

By this hocus-pocus, the King thought that in placing himself under the protection of the Church, the Pope would keep Philip Augustus from striking at England, and the treasonable barons' plot would be foiled.

Now the King felt better, and could give his attention once more to revenge upon those who had incurred his displeasure, promptly forgetting all his pious remorse at having offended God by such acts. There was, first of all, Peter of Pontefract in his dungeon of Corfe Castle. Tomorrow, May 16, was Ascension Day, and John still ruled England. The hermit's prediction had failed to come true.

Not everyone agreed with that, however. There had been those among the immense crowd of spectators on the plain outside Dover Castle who had crossed themselves and murmured how Peter's prediction that before Ascension Day the King would no longer reign, *had* come true with the surrender of his crown to the Pope's representative.

No matter. As Pandulf and his retinue embarked for France, John and his train set out for Dorsetshire. Reaching the town of Wareham, near Corfe Castle, he ordered: "Fetch Peter the Hermit hither."

That day it was the people of Wareham and its vicinity

who were treated to a spectacle. Peter the Hermit and his son, who had been thrown into prison for good measure, were tied to a horse's tail, dragged through the streets of the town and then hanged.

8

Philip Augustus' rage when he learned of John's capitulation to Innocent III was indescribable. He swore that, Pope or no Pope, he would conquer England anyway, and called upon his neighbor, Count Ferrand, ruler of Flanders, for support. When Ferrand refused, having secretly made an alliance with John, the French king invaded the count's little country.

John then sent his fleet out after the French navy. Earl William of Salisbury proved that the King's suspicions were unjust, for he surprised the immense armada of seventeen hundred ships resting at anchor in the port of Damme while the French army was overrunning the rest of Flanders. He fell upon the enemy vessels, captured three hundred and destroyed the rest by setting them afire.

It was a tremendous stroke of fortune for John. Now that he had the support of the powerful Innocent III and the French king was no longer a threat, his worries over his barons' loyalty subsided. If they were inclined to be obedient, all very well; if not, he would crush them.

Now that he was allied with the Church, John set forth to welcome Stephen Langton and the refugees of the English clergy when they landed in England on July 16, 1213. Four days later, before the Cathedral of Winchester, they met. The King advanced toward the exiles, threw himself flat on the ground and burst into tears.

"Have pity upon us and upon England!" he begged.

Perhaps Stephen Langton believed the King's remorse, though it is more likely that he knew the royal character too well and saw only a well-played scene, with John shedding crocodile tears. In any event, he was not going to be diverted from a great purpose with which he had returned to England.

"Before I grant you absolution, Sire," he said, "will you swear to restore the good laws of your ancestors, do away with unjust ones and give all men justice according to the judgment of your court?"

The King swore solemnly that he would do so. Then the archbishop raised him up tenderly, gave him absolution at the cathedral door and led him inside to hear Mass. Afterward there was a great feast at which all rejoiced over the end of the long and bitter quarrel between King and Church.

Determining how much should be paid the Church for its loss of revenues during the five years since John had seized its properties was a very complicated affair. It was finally agreed that John should pay one hundred thousand marks (a mark was two pounds), and make up the difference if the final accounting showed that more was due.

How he was to come by this immense sum did not trouble John in the least. He intended to pay only what he might be forced to, and there was no hurry. At the moment he had more important uses for the money in the royal treasury. Now, he had decided, was the time to strike at France and recover his lost domains there.

He sent out a call to his army to assemble at Portsmouth and embark for France. A rude shock awaited him when he arrived there. The most dissatisfied of his barons, the warlike ones of the North, had ignored the summons. Without them and their knights and soldiers he could not hope to wage an effective campaign in France.

"These base wretches must be punished!" he raved. "It is the law that they owe us service in war!"

"Perhaps they have taken refuge in the claim which has long been made that feudal law does not require the King's vassals to render military service outside the realm, Sire," an aide suggested mildly.

John fixed him with a look that made him shrivel. "It is a part of their treasonable plots against us!" he shouted. "We will march north and destroy them!"

Word of the King's change in plans reached Stephen Langton. He set out after the army and overtook it at Northampton. There, in the castle, he confronted John.

"I have come to dissuade you from this ill-advised action, Sire," he said. "It is in violation of the solemn oath you took at Winchester. You have no right to attack your vassals without a judgment by your court."

"And you," replied John haughtily, "have no right to meddle in affairs which have nothing to do with the Church." And he ordered his army to march on.

Langton followed and had another conference with him. "If you persist in carrying out this plan," he said, "I must warn you I shall see that every member of your army is excommunicated."

His words sobered the malevolent King, who wanted no renewal of his quarrel with the Church, and he abandoned the march.

Stephen Langton was well aware that unless something were done to make the King keep his promises, he would soon forget all of them. The archbishop knew, too, that the barons were in no mood to accept more persecutions. He arranged a meeting with a group of those from the southern part of England at the great church of St. Paul's in London.

"I returned to England in the hope that this country might be restored to an orderly government under the law," he told them. "Otherwise, civil war will surely break out, and the good works of the Church for peace will be lost. You have your grievances. What are they?"

Instantly a hubbub of voices rose, all demanding to be heard. Here and there, Langton made out words and phrases.

"Hostages! . . ."

"A curse on his reliefs and fines!"

"Throw his French jackals out!"

". . . a just price in cash for what he takes of us!"

". . . my daughter . . . sold in marriage to a churlish Frenchman!"

". . . sells justice for what it will bring!"

The archbishop listened in silence as the shouts and maledictions continued. He saw too well that each was thinking only of the injustices which had fallen upon him or his family. Those who had suffered the same wrongs were in agreement; otherwise there was no concern for the others' grievances. Nor were they considering the rights and liberties of the rest of the people, including the clergy of the church he headed in England.

Lack of unity was their chief difficulty. And these men

were all from the South. They rarely saw the northern barons save perhaps in time of war or when a few might serve together as ministers or advisers of the King. Neither group understood the wants and needs of the other.

These men's grievances were just ones, yet the problem, as Langton saw it, was a far greater one: to obtain not only the barons' rights but those of all Englishmen. This was the great hope with which he had returned from France.

The barons needed a leader to unite and guide them. This was the goal, Stephen Langton saw, to which he must devote all his energies and abilities.

"As you know," he finally broke in when the uproar had subsided somewhat, "at Winchester the King swore to restore good laws, abolish bad ones and give every man justice under the law. I have discovered a charter of liberties given by King Henry I to his subjects by which you may, if you will, regain your long-lost rights and your former condition."

A chorus of assent rose among the barons. Most had heard of the charter granted by Henry I, an able ruler and statesman, who had given England good government until his death in 1135. But his successor, King Stephen, had brought ruin and anarchy upon the country in his nineteen-year reign, and the charter had been all but forgotten.

"You must act together if the King is to be brought to restore the charter of Henry I," Langton continued. "If you will do so in defending your rights when the proper time comes, and if necessary die for them, I promise to help you in every way I can."

The proper time, he knew, was not yet. Until it came, he must be satisfied with having implanted the idea of united resistance in the minds of these men.

John raged when he heard what had happened in St. Paul's.

"May twenty thousand devils fly away with this renegade Langton!" he cried. "He must be curbed!" And he dispatched emissaries to the Pope with offerings of money and a letter asking him to restrain the archbishop and to excommunicate the rebellious barons.

Innocent III had been delighted at John's humility in surrendering his crown and acknowledging himself a vassal of the Church of Rome. In spite of the close and lasting bonds of friendship which had been forged between himself and Stephen Langton in their university days, he was annoyed with the archbishop when he received the King's complaint. From then on, Langton's struggle to gain the people of England their rights and liberties was carried on without support from the Church.

John had not given up his plan to invade France and win back Normandy, Aquitaine and the other domains he had lost there. He managed to convince a dozen of the barons who had previously refused to go that they should take part in the venture. The rest still refused.

Nevertheless, the King now had some very powerful allies, including Emperor Otto of the Holy Roman Empire, and the counts of Flanders, Boulogne and Toulouse. Hoping to divide the rest of France among themselves, they agreed to attack from the Northeast while John invaded through the province of Poitou in western France, part of his former great realm of Aquitaine. On February 9, 1214, the King and his army embarked at Portsmouth, sailed to the port of La Rochelle and began their invasion.

For a time all went splendidly. Many of the Poitou nobles joined John's force. The army advanced, taking castle after castle. Possession of all Aquitaine seemed assured.

John sent letters back to the English barons who had remained behind, promising to forgive their rebellious actions if they would come and join him. When they ignored the call, he ordered the justiciar he had left to govern England in his absence to levy the highest scutage that had yet been put upon them.

Then disaster struck. In the Northeast, John's allies were hot in pursuit of Philip Augustus and his army. They caught up with the enemy at the little village of Bouvines.

The French king then turned and fought. In a terrible battle he routed and cut the invaders to pieces and drove the remnant of their army to safety in the Low Countries.

When John heard the news he knew Philip Augustus would lose no time in marching his army west. And he knew that without the aid of his allies he was lost. He moved with all speed to La Rochelle, herded his troops aboard the transports and sailed for home.

In England, when word came of the catastrophe at Bouvines, the barons who had remained behind were jubilant. In John's absence the northern ones had spent their time in plotting revolt. Now the King, having failed miserably to regain his lost possessions in France, would be discredited throughout his kingdom. The time was right for rebellion.

Stephen Langton, too, was heartened. If he could lead the barons, control and keep them from rash action, peace in England might be preserved, and liberty and justice under the law be won.

9

The barons acted quickly but cautiously. Only about forty-five were definitely committed to rebellion, while the total number was close to two hundred. Of those who were not committed, the King could be sure of only a handful as fully loyal, but no one knew what the others would do.

On November 4, 1214, soon after John's ignominious return from France, a group of the rebellious barons, including some from the North, went to Bury St. Edmunds, northeast of London in the county of Suffolk. It was supposed to be a pious pilgrimage, but in the abbey there they did little praying and a great deal of talking about their grievances.

"The Archbishop of Canterbury is right," one of the northern barons finally said. "We must unite and resolve to have justice. Let us take an oath in this holy place that if the King refuses us our rights we will wage war against him. Our first move will be to go to London and demand that King Henry I's charter of liberties be restored."

"I agree," said one of the more timid southern nobles, "but we must be prudent. Let us take the oath, but wait until the Christmas season is past before we go to the King. Meanwhile, what has happened here must be kept a secret."

A majority felt that the delay was advisable. Then they all knelt and took a solemn oath to do as Langton had suggested, and to fight if necessary for their rights.

Like all such secrets, this one soon leaked out. When John heard of the meeting, his anger was tempered with fear, however. Much of his prestige and power had been lost along with the campaign in France. Until he could recover them his best hope lay in intrigue, subterfuge and delay.

He dispatched an emissary to the Pope, begging for support. At the same time he sent an urgent message to one of the most powerful of his French allies in Poitou, Savaric de Mauléon, urging him to come to England with a force of soldiers.

John planned to spend the Christmas season at his castle in Worcester. Formerly, none of the barons who were invited each year for the royal holiday festivities had dared stay away, but this Christmas in 1214 was dismal indeed for the King. When only a few nobles appeared, he demanded to know why. No one seemed to know.

His ministers, among the few loyal barons who gathered at the castle, had news that sent the King into one of his uncontrollable rages.

"The royal treasury is almost empty, Sire," Richard Marsh, now John's chancellor, informed him. "The expenses for the campaign in France were very heavy. . . ."

"Then find more money!" John screamed at him. "What of the scutage we levied upon those who refused us service in France?"

"Your demands for payment have been largely ignored, my liege," replied his Treasurer of the Exchequer, William of Ely.

"What of our sheriffs?" stormed the King. "We pay them handsomely to collect our taxes. Where is the money?"

"They are having . . . difficulties, Sire," said Marsh.

"Let them arrest and throw the debtors in prison! Impose more fines! Seize the lands!"

His advisers forbore to tell the quivering monarch that obedience to his commands seemed to have broken down all over England.

The King snatched up a roll of parchment that lay before him. "Is this some jest?" he stormed. "A demand that we receive a group of our barons to hear what they call their 'just grievances' . . . signed by FitzWalter . . . Mowbray . . . Bigod . . . Mandeville . . . and the rest . . . traitors all! We'll see them swing from a gallows tree first! . . ."

In spite of his bluster he was frightened, and he agreed to meet the rebellious barons at the Temple in London on January 6, 1215. Nevertheless he was determined to reveal no sign of weakness that might encourage them to harden their stand.

Facing them, he spoke in a surly voice: "What manner of address is this from vassals who demand an audience with us, your liege lord?"

FitzWalter was their spokesman: "We meant no disrespect, Sire, but only to assert our lawful right to a hearing for our plaints." The words were polite, but the tone was unyielding.

"Lawful!" John exploded. "It is for us to decide what is lawful in our kingdom. We remind you of our duty to suppress treasonable actions by force. . . ."

"Force," said FitzWalter, "may be met by force, my liege."

Confronting the bold-faced, uncompromising men, John saw he had better control his temper. "What are these so-called demands of yours?" he asked.

"That you confirm the good laws which King Edward established after his conquest of the kingdom, and restore the charter of liberties given to his subjects by King Henry I."

Denying their petition might bring on immediate civil war, John saw. "This is a grave matter," he told them. "We must have time to study this charter and consider its provisions. Many years have passed since it was granted . . . times have changed."

He wondered how much grace they would allow him. "We will give you our answer the Monday after Easter," he said, and added quickly, "Be assured that your just grievances will be fully satisfied."

Reluctantly the barons agreed. As for the King, in the precious time gained, he fortified and protected himself in every way he could.

First, he commanded the sheriffs of every county in England to administer a new, strongly worded oath of allegiance to all his subjects. They were to swear to stand with the King against all men. At the same time he sent to Poitou for more troops.

Most of all, he counted upon the support of the Church. When he learned that the rebels had sent Eustace de Vesci to Rome with a plea that the Pope compel him to meet their demands, John devised a scheme to counter the move. On March 4 he took a vow to go on a crusade.

It was a clever ruse. He had not the slightest intention of going off to the Holy Land, but by taking the vow he became entitled to Rome's protection. Thus if the barons rose against him they would be defying the Church and the Pope.

Meanwhile, Innocent III wrote three letters to England. One, to Stephen Langton, said that his Holiness was greatly shocked to learn that his Archbishop of Canterbury favored the barons. He told Langton to work for peace, and to excommunicate all barons who conspired against John. At the same time he wrote the barons, ordering them to pay the hated scutage, and said they might request the King to accede to their demands, but must do so politely. The third letter, to John, urged him to grant any "just petitions" of the barons.

The King was convinced that the Pope was on his side, that with the aid of the barons who were still loyal and their knights, and with that of the soldiers from Poitou, he could control any uprising. On April 13, when he met with a group of the rebels at Oxford, he continued to shilly-shally and evade their demands.

The barons then took threatening action, but the King still did not believe they really meant it. A courier, galloping in from Northamptonshire, brought the word: "The rebels have assembled under arms at Stamford."

Armed force . . . it was a bluff, John decided. He called on the most faithful of all his barons, William Marshal. "Go and see what it is these traitors want," he commanded. "Have them give you a list of their demands. And take the Archbishop of Canterbury with you. They will listen to him."

Obedient to the Pope's order to work for peace, Langton went along with Marshal. They found the rebels at the town of Brackley.

"It is the King's desire that your grievances be settled peaceably," Marshal told the leaders of the revolt. "He has sent us to obtain from you the exact reforms you wish granted."

Langton assured the rebels that he would use his influence to see that they were given justice.

"We will draw up a list of our demands," replied Fitz-Walter. His gaze was grim and unflinching. "We, too, desire a peaceable settlement—but we trust the King will immediately put his agreement in writing and affix his royal seal to it, thus averting seizure of his castles, lands and goods."

Marshal and Langton took the demands to the King at Windsor Castle and informed him of the barons' ultimatum. The list consisted chiefly of such of the old laws and customs, granted in earlier times but ignored by John and his brother Richard, which the rebels now wanted restored.

When the King had read them he exploded into a towering rage. "Why do not these barons, with their unjust exactions, demand our kingdom?" he shouted, and swore a fearful oath. "We will never grant them such liberties as will make a slave of us!"

Marshal and Langton bore the refusal back to Brackley. The rebels then held a meeting and chose the former outlaw and exile, Robert FitzWalter, as their commander. They gave him the pious title of "Marshal of the host of God and Holy Church."

FitzWalter ordered his force to march to Northampton and lay siege to the King's great castle there. The barons' revolt had begun, but even then John refused to take it too seriously. During the siege he sent a peace proposal, offering to submit the barons' grievances to arbitration by the Pope. He did so only to gain time, for he was still assembling his military forces. The offer was indignantly rejected, for the barons feared Innocent III would favor John too heavily.

Reports from Northampton made John a little contemptuous of his enemies. His fortress there was powerful and strongly defended. The rebels, with their hastily assembled army, were not equipped for an assault upon it.

To batter down the walls of such a stronghold, the engines of destruction known as catapults were needed. They could hurl rocks and millstones weighing two or three hundred pounds a distance of three hundred yards at battlements or into castle moats, filling them up so the besiegers could cross. Or a great tower, called a beffroy, might be moved against the walls, permitting the invaders to scale them.

FitzWalter had none of these. After two weeks he had to give up the siege. His army then moved to Brackley, where it had the rather dubious satisfaction of taking the weakly defended and second-rate castle there.

King John was heartened, but at last he had made a fatal mistake. He had dallied too long. During the second week of May a disturbing report reached him: "A revolt, led by three of the rebel barons, has begun in Devonshire."

John had two faithful barons in that southwestern county, Henry de Pomeroy and John de Erley. He appointed them joint sheriffs and ordered them to put down the revolt. Then more disquieting intelligence reached him.

"The rebels are negotiating with the citizens of London to yield up the city," he was told.

This was serious. London was not only by far the largest city in England, but the wealthiest, the center of English trade. It was governed by a lord mayor appointed by the King, with two sheriffs to administer the laws and collect taxes. But now the real power to determine what would happen to London in a civil war lay with the citizens.

Although the King had his friends among the rich merchants and officials of the city government, these were a handful compared to the great mass of the common people, fiercely independent, united against John's tyrannies and ripe for revolt if someone stood ready to lead them. Practically all of the loyal barons had their castles in other parts of England. The King's palace of Westminster lay outside the walls, and his only military strength within the city was the small garrison in the Tower of London. Unless he could place a powerful armed force in London, the rebels, having the good will of the citizens, would have little trouble in seizing the city.

John called in the Earl of Salisbury. "Take a force and march to London," he said. "The city must not be surrendered!" Next day he ordered the archdeacon of Huntingdon, a member of one of the few London baronial families, the powerful Cornhills, to the capital to use his influence with the people.

He also threw a sop to the inhabitants of the city. The independent-minded Londoners resented having their mayor appointed by the King to serve for his whole lifetime. Now John gave them a new charter, allowing them to elect their own mayor, and to get rid of him after one year by choosing a new one if they wished.

All this was too late. Darkness still shrouded London on Sunday morning, May 17, when a column of mailclad knights on their armored horses, followed by the foot soldiers of Robert FitzWalter's little army, came over the steep slope of Holborn. As they approached the western entrance in the city's walls known as Newgate, there was no sound save the steady beat of hoofs, the tramp of feet and the clank of metal on metal as the riders swayed in their saddles.

Outside the gate the column halted. An aide dismounted, went up to it and was back in a moment to report to Fitz-Walter: "Open, as promised, my Lord."

FitzWalter turned and spoke in a low voice to those behind him: "If we are attacked, we fight. But no man shall draw bowstring against a citizen. They are to plunder only when given permission to enter the houses of those known to support the King." He raised his hand over his head. "Forward!"

It was done quickly and without a fight. Only curious stares and an occasional friendly hail from early risers greeted the army as it followed its leaders across the city in the dawn. It passed the grim pile of Newgate Prison, the slaughter-houses of Fleshshambles Street, already astir, the silent shops of West Chepe, traversed Cornhill and reached the gateway of the Tower of London, just inside the east wall.

There the column stopped again. The great keep of the fortress rose before them with its four high, peak-roofed towers. A demand for surrender was sent in, and a prompt refusal returned.

"We can hold the city without the Tower," said Fitz-Walter. "Its garrison is small and an attack will mean a loss of men and animals, neither of which we can afford."

As the sun rose over the Tower and the battlements of the east wall, the soldiers fanned out through the streets. London was stirring, for Sunday was market day, a time when those who worked through the week could go shopping.

Many among FitzWalter's troops had never before seen the vast metropolis with its thirty-five thousand inhabitants, and they gazed in stupefaction at its sights and sounds. They shouldered their way through market-bound throngs jamming streets in which the gabled, projecting upper stories of the houses almost touched each other, and looked like gossips leaning out to whisper scandal across the narrow thoroughfares.

The soldiers made eyes at pretty girls and young housewives, who giggled as they pretended not to see. Their noses wrinkled as they caught the stench from the filth-choked little Fleet River that flowed into the Thames, and that from the gutters in the middle of the streets, where kites and crows gabbled and fought over garbage and the carcasses of dead dogs and cats. From the taverns with their signs bearing names like Pope's Head and Cardinal's Hat came odors that were more savory, and the clatter of alepots and platters to whet appetites already made sharp by hawkers' street cries dinning into their ears: "Hot peasecods!" "Hot pies, hot!" "Hot sheep's feet!"

They stared in awe at the great houses of the rich, and true to FitzWalter's promise they were allowed to enter those of known friends to the King. Charging in, they sent haughty lords and their elegant ladies scrambling helter-skelter for their lives. They gleefully smashed furniture to kindling, and emerged laden with all sorts of silly trophies which would be thrown away as soon they grew too heavy to carry.

Save for the Tower, over which a banner emblazoned with the arms of John of England floated, the city had fallen to the rebels with the aid and blessing of its citizens who were friendly to their cause. Foolishly, the King had sent the Earl of Salisbury and his troops to Devonshire, for reports of the uprising there had become ominous.

The news of London's capture was a blow to John. Then to add to his worries came word from Devonshire that Salisbury had retreated ignominiously without firing a shot when he heard that the rebels there were very strong. The King ordered his relative to go back and fight, and then turned his attention to what he should do about the barons in London.

He summoned Stephen Langton to his castle at Windsor. "There was no need for our dissatisfied barons to take arms

A Knight and Noble Ladies

Peasants and Warriors

against us," he told the archbishop. "We had already signified our readiness to grant their reasonable demands."

Was John really ready to give the barons what they wanted? Or was this some sort of treachery? Well as he knew the King and his ways, Stephen Langton was himself no man of intrigue, nor was he a soldier. It seemed reasonable that since the rebels held the great metropolis of London, and John's prestige and military strength had been weakened by the defeat in France, he was ready to yield.

Still wary, however, he said, "The barons have already refused to accept arbitration of their demands by the Holy Father in Rome, Sire. I do not believe they will change their minds."

"Then let a conference be arranged between us," John suggested. "Their just grievances shall be satisfied."

Langton's heart leaped with hope. His position was a difficult one. The letter he had received from the Pope had placed him on the King's side, whether he liked it or not. He was to work for peace, and Innocent III had made it plain that he must not support the barons. But if John were sincere in his offer, Langton might be able to guide the barons in their demands and bring about the great purpose which was so close to his heart.

"I will try to arrange the conference," he promised.

"In the meantime," continued the King, "there must be a truce. If this is agreeable to the barons, I will order my officers to observe it."

Langton went to FitzWalter and the other rebel leaders in London, and told them of his interview. "I believe the King is ready to grant your just demands," he said.

FitzWalter was less trustful than the archbishop. "Very well," he replied, "we will negotiate with him. And we agree to the truce, but our army will go with us to the conference, just in case. . . ."

"First," interposed the archbishop, "you must all set to work in preparing your demands. There is much to be done before you meet with the King."

"But you and my Lord Marshal submitted our demands to him while we were at Brackley—" FitzWalter began.

"And they were rejected in scorn," Langton reminded him. "You must go over them with care, revising and re-grouping them so that the meaning of each will be fully clear. You must also consider whether some should be left out or altered so they will be acceptable to the King, and whether some new ones should be included."

While he was no political schemer, Stephen Langton spoke as a master diplomat. He had said nothing of himself. It was "you must do this," and "you must do that."

Yet he knew perfectly well that the barons themselves could never put their demands into a form which would make this the great document he hoped for. Except for a very few, these were uneducated men. A good many could not even sign their own names. None were scholars like himself. Langton knew that the handful of intelligent men among them would see that they needed his help in drafting this charter of liberties. But by saying they were the ones who must do it, he flattered and pleased them.

The archbishop had already done much thinking about the form the charter must take. Throughout his career, the principle he had put into words years before in the lecture to his students at the Sorbonne had stood before him like a shining grail: "The subject owes obedience only as long as the King acts according to law, and upon the advice of his proper counselors."

As he thought it over, it all came down to a simple phrase: *The King is not above the law.*

This was the great underlying principle upon which the charter of liberties must be founded as a cornerstone of English law.

Just as Langton had surmised, FitzWalter now said, "We pray you, my Lord Archbishop, to give us your help in drafting the charter of liberties."

"I will give you whatever advice and counsel you desire, my Lord Robert," Langton agreed. "But you will need time for this work—a fortnight at the least."

"Then," said the rebel leader, "let the King and his advisers meet us in the meadow of Runnymede by the Thames below his castle of Windsor on the fifteenth of June."

10

It was fortunate that the rebellious barons had asked Stephen Langton to act as their adviser in drawing up the charter of liberties. As these quarrelsome and selfish men set to work, each wanted his own particular grievance considered first. Without the archbishop to bring order out of chaos, they might well have fallen into such wrangling that the charter would never have been drafted in the form which was to make it a great and lasting document.

They respected Langton's learning, however, and his calm, considered judgment. They listened to his counsel. Wisely, he let them discuss first the grievances which affected the greatest number. As for his own ideas, he would bide his time and bring each up at the proper moment.

When it came to the most hated of all John's tyrannies, the voices of a substantial number of the rebel barons rose above the rest.

"By the rood! let him first give up our sons he has taken, and swear to forbear evermore from demanding hostages of us! There must be no more of it!" Roger de Cressi's voice was loudest of all, and with good reason, for only a few days ago the avenging King had seized his son.

There was a chorus of assent from the others who had been forced to surrender their sons, as well as from William Marshal, the younger, who himself had once been a hostage, and whose father, now reconciled with John, was the most loyal of the few who still supported the King.

Next to the safety of the hostages the King had taken, solicitude for their lands lay closest to the barons' hearts.

"He must give back our property he seized after we took arms against him!" cried William de Mandeville, whose demand was instantly supported by shouts from the entire company, for since the rebellious barons had assembled under arms at Stamford, the manors and castles of most had been overrun by the King's men, while some had had lands taken at other times during John's reign.

"What of us whose backs he has broken with his villainous reliefs?" growled Nicholas de Stutville. He was speaking of the sum of money, determined by the King, which feudal custom required an heir to pay when he took possession of his late father's property and assumed his title. "I paid ten thousand marks for the lands my brother left me, and my own barony of Knaresborough. Is he to continue these robberies which put highwaymen to shame?"

"Aye, faith!" Peter de Bruce chimed in. "I, too, paid him tribute in excess of all reason to regain a small barony. A thousand pounds, by my hilt! Nor will the manor's revenues pay the debt and dribble a penny of profit into my pockets if I live to the age of the patriarch Methuselah!"

"I paid a thousand marks for mine!" cried Robert de Vere, Earl of Oxford.

"Aye!" a young man shouted, "there is no limit to his greed. I am here to represent the family of FitzAlan. The King demanded twenty thousand pounds of my older brother William for my late father's modest baronies of Clun and Whitchurch. Yet I am told that in the time of King Henry II the usual relief for such baronies was a thousand pounds."

"Do you know why such an enormous sum was demanded?" Langton asked.

"Aye, my Lord Archbishop. When my father was in the King's favor he was sheriff of Shropshire. Many of his knights were friends of the worthy Fulk FitzWarin, who is among us today and can testify to what I say. Believing that my father also supported FitzWarin, the King removed him as sheriff. He could do him no more harm at the time, but he took revenge upon the heir, my brother, when my father died."

"Was the relief paid?" the archbishop pursued.

FitzAlan made a helpless gesture. "My brother could not possibly raise the money. The lands are still held by Thomas de Eardington, my father's successor as sheriff, whom the King appointed custodian of the property as my brother's guardian under the law."

Another young nobleman rose. "A curse on his guardianships! My father also fell out with the King. When he died, as the eldest son I was his heir. Since like William FitzAlan I was not yet twenty-one, the King became my guardian, too, charged with administering the estate until I was of age. He sold the privilege to one of his French favorites, who has ruined the property."

"Ruined, you say?" queried Langton.

"The King's custodian stripped it of all that was of value —its woodland cut down and sold for timber, horses, cattle, sheep, swine and poultry fetched to market, even the hay in the barns. Fields supposed to lie fallow for a season were sowed with the rest until the soil's fertility was exhausted."

Growls and mutterings went up from the group, indicating that others were familiar with the King's practice of selling guardianships to the highest bidder, who then plundered the property.

"And that was not the end of it, my Lord Archbishop," the young baron continued. "When I came of age, the King demanded an exorbitant relief."

"You paid it?" Langton asked.

The baron threw up his hands. "What else could I do? Otherwise my title of nobility would have been lost. By my faith, it will be years before I can restore the manor to its former prosperity, many more until it produces enough to pay off the relief. Meanwhile, if I do not meet the payments, the King may seize my lands, cast me into prison or cause me to bear the wolf's-head."

"What say you who have fallen from the King's grace and bought it back at his ruinous rates for benevolence?" Roger de Cressi asked of the others. "Let me speak first of this. Many of you know how, when I sought to marry, he refused permission, having other plans for the lady to the fattening of his purse. Like any lover whose blood flows red in his veins, I scorned his forbiddance and married her, whereupon he seized the lands of my modest barony, as well as hers, until I paid him twelve hundred marks and two saddle horses."

"By my soul, you were lucky!" shouted Robert de Vaux. "He did not cast you into one of his foul dungeons as he did me when, without a jot of evidence, I was suspected of plotting against him. I paid two thousand marks for my freedom and his grace!"

At this point, Stephen Langton saw his opportunity to speak for all the people.

"My lords, this is a just grievance and a weighty one, for not only you but a great host of your vassals have long suffered the injustice of immoderate fines and amercements imposed upon them to increase the royal revenues." By amercements the archbishop was referring to what are known today as fines, penalties imposed in court for misdeeds, whereas in those times a fine was a gift, supposed to be given voluntarily in return for a favor from the King or to patch up a quarrel with him. "In writing your demands, I beseech you to remember that all subjects should be protected against tyranny."

Another matter close to the archbishop's heart then came up for discussion. A hulking, black-browed knight stood forth.

"I speak for all who have suffered the persecutions of this tyrant without due process of law!" His scowling gaze swept the assemblage. "You have all seen them; more than one has felt them. You, Robert FitzWalter, and you, Eustace de Vesci, were forced to flee the country; you, Robert de Vaux, were cast into prison—and I, Fulk FitzWarin, have borne the wolf's-head!"

The former outlaw stood glowering, the one man among them who had personally forced the King to revoke one of his savage punishments. Then Giles de Briouse rose.

"Aye, Sir Fulk!" he cried, "and I speak for my father, driven from the kingdom to die in France, and for my mother and brother who perished miserably at his hands in the keep of Windsor! A pity their shades cannot appear to tell what they suffered!"

"Or the spirit of Geoffrey, the clerk of the Exchequer," added Stephen Langton. "You will deliberate no greater injustice upon English subjects of all degree than this one, my lords. Therefore, do not forget, I pray you in the name of God and Holy Church, that they—and among them the clergy —have also suffered these persecutions."

The archbishop then interposed a question: "My lords, have you considered how this and other sections of the charter of liberties are to be enforced?"

His words stilled the hubbub of voices about him. Absorbed in discussing their demands, they had forgotten this all-important point. How, indeed, was the shifty and treacherous king to be made to keep his promises?

One of the rebel leaders shouted, "We have a remedy, my Lord Archbishop!" His hand flew to the hilt of his sword, and with a flourish he drew the weapon and held it flashing aloft. "There is our remedy!"

"No, my lord," said Langton quietly. "When we met in London to consider your grievances, I told you I had returned to England in the hope that orderly government under the law might be restored. This charter of liberties must be the foundation of the law by which we may have orderly government."

He paused while his eyes swept the faces before him. At the sight of so much ferocity, greed and selfishness his heart quailed. How was he to make them understand the importance of the great principle for which he was striving?

"The King has set himself above the law," he went on. "All of your grievances have arisen because he has ignored the ancient laws and customs of England. By this charter you must make certain that henceforth he shall act under the law. But you must find orderly means of enforcing the charter if it is to be the cornerstone of the law. You must use arms only as a last resort."

As Langton concluded he felt that his words had made an impression, and he was heartened.

"How are we to make the King obey the charter, my Lord Archbishop?" one of the leaders asked. "We cannot bring him to answer before a court, for he is able to control his justices."

"Then you must appoint men to enforce it whom the King cannot control," replied Langton.

"He cannot control us," said one of the barons. "Let us name twenty-five of our number to administer the charter."

Another objected: "Our castles and manors are spread wide over all England. It will be difficult to assemble such a large group every time a dispute occurs."

"Then let a small number of the group be empowered to hear complaints of violations," said the first baron. "These men can go to the King, or his justiciar if he is away, and ask that the matter be corrected. If it is refused, the whole group can meet to consider it."

He turned to Langton: "Do you not agree this is the best way, my Lord Archbishop?"

Langton hesitated. He saw that the King would be no more willing to allow the rebel barons to enforce the charter than they were to have John's justices do so. And in truth, such an arrangement would tend to give them too much power. The best way would be to have a small group of men of integrity and ability who would not be partial toward either side in their deliberations.

The rebel barons, he believed, might accept him as one of

such a group, but there would have to be others. He thought of William Marshal, the elder. Marshal was a man of stature and intelligence, and he was incorruptible. But he was now the King's chief ally. The rebels would never accept him or any other barons outside their own ranks. No, it would be best to go along with their plan, and pray that somehow it might work.

"It would seem that your suggestion is worthy of consideration," he told the baron who had proposed it. To the whole group he said, "If those who administer the charter wish my advice upon any matter, I am at their service, my lords."

"And if a violation is brought before the full group and they, too, fail to make the King obey? . . ." one of them began.

"Then," said Langton, "if the complaint is a lawful one, you will be justified in waging war upon him until he complies." And he repeated the words, ever fresh in his mind, which he had spoken years before to his class at the Sorbonne: "The subject owes obedience only as long as the king acts according to law, and upon the advice of his proper counselors." He added, "Those who are appointed to see that the King acts according to law will be his proper counselors. If he then refuses, you will have no choice but force of arms."

The barons forgot none of their grievances as they continued their discussion and gradually reached agreement as to what should be included in their demands. They were based first of all upon the charter of liberties granted by King Henry I, but some parts were revised, and other measures added. Stephen Langton used his influence judiciously. He cautioned the barons when their indignation against the King led them toward unfair retaliation, and injected suggestions for provisions which would guarantee the common people and clergy their rights and liberties as well as the barons.

The rebels were agreed that the detested levying of exorbitant scutages and certain other taxes must be controlled. So must the evils of purveyance. As for the forest laws, the injustices the King had practiced throughout his reign should be ended.

There was more discussion of the King's seizure of lands and goods, for he had taken them unlawfully not only to punish his enemies, but to enrich himself at the expense of debtors to the Crown, of convicted felons and of widows whose inheritances he denied them. When the subject of widows came up, complaints were also freely voiced of how John had often forced them, as well as attractive and wealthy maidens, to marry men who had paid him well for the privilege.

One of the injustices which especially outraged the barons was the King's practice of giving fat jobs to favorites he had invited to England from France. Not only did it rob Englishmen of these posts, but many of the usurpers named as royal officers knew nothing of the law and cared less about enforcing it justly. As for the foreign troops John had summoned from France to fight against his enemies, they must go.

One subject which Stephen Langton brought up, the barons did not like.

"If the King is to agree to observe faithfully all the provisions of the charter of liberties, you must also promise to observe them faithfully," he reminded them.

He saw frowns and scowls on the faces about him. It had not occurred to them until then that if the charter were to be the cornerstone of orderly government and law, it must be obeyed by all.

"As vassals of the King, you will expect him to obey the charter," Langton went on. "If he does not, you will be forced to fight for your rights. The same will hold true of those who are your vassals. And you will never enjoy the support of the Church unless these privileges are also extended to all the clergy."

They saw that the archbishop was right; that they could not hope for the support of those who served them, as they served the King, unless the provisions of the charter included their vassals. If there were to be any prospect that Rome would approve of the charter, they must also insure the freedoms of the Church.

The barons agreed to Langton's suggestion, perhaps with a little too much celerity for his peace of mind, since he was adept at reading men's true motives.

Thus at last, as the fifteenth of June approached, the grievances of the barons were put upon parchment in a document known as the "Articles of the Barons." This was the charter whose principles John of England must accept in the meadow of Runnymede.

On the whole, Stephen Langton was satisfied. It was far from a perfect document, he knew. He had had to be cautious in using pressure upon the barons in order to gain his objectives lest they think he was trying to dictate to them. But at Runnymede, if indeed the King did not hurl the charter into the faces of his enemies, there must be much negotiation before the royal seal could be affixed to it. Perhaps some of the sections of the Articles of the Barons would be modified and improved then.

The one provision which disturbed the archbishop most was that which set up the group of twenty-five barons to enforce the charter. He doubted that the King would accept it.

If he did so, it would be only because he was forced to it. It meant that twenty-five barons stood above the ruler. John would never submit to such humiliation; the moment he was strong enough he would resist, and civil war would result. Thus Langton's cherished orderly government under the law would not be achieved.

If he could have known what was in the minds of the King and the rebel barons alike as the day of Runnymede neared, his uneasiness would have turned to alarm and dread.

11

The trumpets blared and the barons cantered forward. As they moved over the long sweep of the meadow of Runnymede beside the placid river, ring mail, swords, lances, shields and spurs flickered and flashed in the glancing morning sunlight. Against the greensward many colors stood out in brilliant contrast—those of the riders' surcoats, the horses' trappings, and the pennons and banners emblazoned with armorial bearings which fluttered in the breeze.

The advancing front of the more than twoscore noblemen stretched across the width of the meadow. There in the center, Robert FitzWalter sat his steed arrogantly, his eyes as adamant as the steel of the hauberk covering his white surcoat. Beside him rode Eustace de Vesci, his bearing also haughty and vengeful. During their exile both men had dreamed of such a day as this fifteenth of June, 1215.

All were there, these rebels who had drawn up the Articles of the Barons—the great Earls of Norfolk, Hertford, Essex,

Oxford, Hereford and Winchester, the Barons de Lacy, de Bruce, de Percy, de Stutville, the scowling, once-outlawed FitzWarin, and the rest. All kept their eyes fixed straight upon their objective at the opposite end of the field.

Approaching it, FitzWalter raised his hand in signal. All drew up, dismounted, turned their horses over to attendants who had followed, and advanced on foot, striding clumsily in their armor.

Then, as FitzWalter came face to face with the short, broad-shouldered man standing slightly ahead of the party waiting there, they halted. All up and down the long line, heads turned expectantly toward the center. Would their leader kneel?

FitzWalter did not. He merely proffered the roll of parchment to the King. "Here, Sire, are the demands which you have signified you are willing to grant us."

From the voluminous sleeves of his crimson tunic, John extended a hand encased in a jeweled glove and took the Articles of the Barons. Only by a herculean effort was he able to carry off the humiliation he had just received. As he looked up and down the line of stalwart, ruffianly men with eyes like falcons, his fingers itched to feel their throats in his grip. But he controlled himself, for he had only to shift his gaze beyond the long rank of the barons to know how helpless he was.

There at the upper end of the meadow the rebel army of knights, foot soldiers and crossbowmen was massed. All stood motionless, but their very immobility spelled readiness, and this was heightened when, here and there, a knight's charger pawed the turf impatiently. The King knew FitzWalter had only to turn and raise his arm to bring down the might of that phalanx upon him and his party.

Thus, to the rebel barons, John's rage was not visible. They had humbled him, yet in the figure standing before them they saw only imperiousness. It was there in the bold and cruel eyes, in the proud carriage, in the way his white mantle was flung carelessly open over one shoulder, exposing its lining of vair.

"It is true," he said, "that for the sake of peace and the good of our kingdom, we are willing to grant certain laws and liberties. . . . But we sent word to you at Brackley by our venerated Archbishop of Canterbury and our faithful Earl of Pembroke that we would never grant you such liberties as would make us your slave. These matters must be discussed and considered by us and the advisers who have come here with us today."

John turned slightly and made a sweeping gesture which encompassed the party behind him. These were the men who had proved the King's staunch supporters in the face of all his transgressions. First among them in loyalty and devotion was William Marshal, Earl of Pembroke. For six years he had suffered the bitter enmity of the suspicious monarch until John had deigned to forgive him. Marshal knew the royal character well, yet his high sense of duty had impelled him to stand by his master.

Among the rest were the Earls of Surrey, Arundel and Salisbury, and such lesser nobles as Warin FitzGerold, Peter FitzHerbert, Hubert de Burgh, Hugh de Neville and William Marshal's nephew John. Of fair treatment at their hands, FitzWalter and his men might be less sure than with the elder Marshal. On the other hand these barons, like themselves, held their own interests of first importance; it was not impossible that some might yet desert the King if it proved to their advantage.

Except for Stephen Langton, the rebels had little hope of support from the delegation of the clergy. John had not overlooked the importance of having an impressive group to represent his ally, the Church, for its presence might curb his enemies' vengefulness. Led by Langton and arrayed in all the splendor of bejeweled miter and crozier, and silken, gold-embroidered vestments, they included the Archbishop of Dublin and the Bishops of London, Winchester, Bath, Lincoln, Worcester, Coventry and Rochester. To protect the interests of Rome itself was that adroit diplomat, the Cardinal Pandulf, while the influential order of the Knights Templar was represented by its master in England, Brother Aymeric.

With another wave of his hand, King John ushered Fitz-Walter toward a great peak-roofed tent which had been erected on the field. The other rebel leaders and the royal train followed.

Inside the tent, tables consisting of boards laid upon trestles had been set up. At one a battery of royal clerks in their priestly and monkish robes sat perched on stools with parchment, ink and quills before them.

The two delegations ranged themselves about the other tables, and the deliberations began. John handed the Articles of the Barons to one of his clerks, who began to read it aloud. In turn each clause of the Articles was taken up and discussed by the negotiators. As Langton had feared, John raised a storm of objections to almost every one. Yet the archbishop was surprised when, by the time long shadows had begun to steal over the meadow of Runnymede in the late afternoon, the King had agreed in principle to the barons' demands.

In the quarters provided for him at Windsor Castle after the meeting had been adjourned for the day, Langton discussed the proceedings with William de Sainte-Mère-Église, Bishop of London, who had been one of his companions in exile in France during John's quarrel with the Church.

Relaxing in a chair, he passed his hand over his forehead. "It has been a wearing day, William," he said.

"Ah, yes," replied the bishop, "your skill as a peacemaker and counselor was more than once severely tried, my Lord Archbishop. Whenever his Majesty's hackles rose like those of an embattled rooster, it was only your logical and persuasive arguments which soothed him."

"I am grateful to you for your assistance, as well as to the rest of our clergy who were present," said Langton.

Before replying, Sainte-Mère-Église looked over his shoulder and lowered his voice as though he feared someone might be listening. "I must acknowledge that the provisions of the Articles which concede the clergy their rights were pleasing to me," he said then, adding, "and to the rest, I am sure. Naturally, being heedful of the Holy Father's opposition to the rebellious barons, caution was necessary. . . ."

"At least, William, you and others supported me by your silence when the King disputed provisions I felt should be retained for the good of all in the kingdom." And with a chuckle, the archbishop added, "Nor did I hear objections from the barons of the King's train to provisions which are to the advantage of all English noblemen. But I was most grateful for the support of my Lord Pembroke upon several points which can benefit him little."

"He is a man of character," said the bishop. Again he spoke softly: "If the King were like William Marshal, all the troubles which have beset Holy Church and the kingdom could have been avoided." He shook his head. "It is a wonder to me that, in spite of his weakened position, his Majesty granted all the demands. I thought he would stalk from the council tent when the provision for the twenty-five barons to enforce the charter was brought up."

Langton smiled. "So did I, William. Perhaps he was kept from it by the barons' wisdom in stipulating that if they are forced to make war it will not be upon his person or his family. In that way they avoided asserting direct power over him."

"Or perhaps," said Sainte-Mère-Église dryly, "it was the thought of the barons' army outside in the meadow. . . . Nevertheless, I was surprised at his docility."

"And I too," agreed Langton. "Sometimes I wonder what plans may be unfolding in his head. . . ." He rose from his chair and slowly paced across the chamber and back before he spoke again: "Much depends upon his actions after the charter is issued. If he lives up to its provisions, the people will enjoy liberties such as they have known under no other ruler of England—but if he does not, the kingdom will sink into the slough of civil war and anarchy."

With a sigh he sat down again. "At least it has been a day of accomplishment, now that the King has affixed his great seal to the Articles of the Barons as a basis for the final charter. We shall be occupied for several days yet, however. There are questions still in dispute to be settled, and the proposed new provisions to be drafted. It will be a busy time."

June 15, 1215, was a Monday. The next three days were devoted to settling the disputed questions, the writing of new sections and assembling the clauses into logical order. As Stephen Langton had prophesied, it was a busy time for all, especially the clerks, whose quills flew unceasingly over the long sheets of parchment. Some took down the changes and additions as they were dictated, while others labored on revision and rearrangement, and to smooth out the language of the charter.

At last, on Friday, June 19, the document known as Magna Carta or the Great Charter was ready. There had been forty-nine clauses in the Articles of the Barons. In the new charter some of these had been split up into more than one section, and with the additions, Magna Carta had sixty-three clauses or chapters as they are generally called.

Of those which still stand today as pillars of liberty for free men, perhaps the most important of all was Chapter 39:

No free man shall be taken or imprisoned or disseized (*his property taken from him*) or exiled or in any way destroyed, nor will we go upon him nor send upon him, except by the lawful judgment of his peers and by the law of the land.

Chapter 39 meant that never again should such men and women as William and Matilda de Briouse and their eldest son, or Fulk FitzWarin, the clerk Geoffrey, Robert FitzWalter and Eustace de Vesci be outlawed, forced to flee the country or allowed to waste away and die miserably in some loathsome dungeon without first being given a fair trial conducted in accordance with the law, and by the judgment of their equals. Nor would the King be permitted again to seize property unlawfully.

Wretched persons like Godiva Basset were no longer to be at the mercy of sheriffs and other court officials who had forced them to undergo the dread ordeals without a chance to prove their innocence by the testimony of witnesses. Another of Magna Carta's famous and enduring provisions, Chapter 38, stated:

No bailiff for the future shall, upon his own unsupported complaint, put anyone to his law without credible witnesses brought for this purpose.

Not only did sheriffs and other royal officers break ancient law by denying to an accused person the right to call witnesses. A man summoned before a county court and charged with a serious crime never knew whether the case would be put aside to await the arrival of the King's itinerant justices as the law required, or whether the sheriff might arrogantly refuse him the right of a "plea of the Crown," and try the case himself. Another important clause, in Chapter 24, read:

No sheriff, constable, coroner or others of our bailiffs, shall hold pleas of the Crown.

If a man brought suit against another in a dispute over land, it was known as a "common plea," and had to be heard by another royal court. Since the King was forever on the move, and these justices traveled with him, more than one English subject had chased them for weeks and even months over the length and breadth of England and even abroad before catching up with them. Chapter 17 ordered that these courts sit in a fixed place.

Chapter 36 of the Great Charter forbade the King to sell writs of inquisition of life or limb, without which innocent persons accused of murder were refused the right to have witnesses testify for them, and thus might lose their lives by being put to the ordeal by combat:

Nothing in future shall be given or taken for a writ of inquisition of life or limb, but freely it shall be granted, and never denied.

The barons wanted to make certain that John should not find ways to refuse prompt justice to anyone, perhaps by selling other necessary documents, or by allowing accused persons to languish in prison for weeks or months without being brought to trial. Therefore, in Chapter 40, they had inserted a second provision covering justice:

To no one will we sell, to no one will we refuse or delay, right or justice.

The King's practice of insuring the barons' loyalty by holding their sons as hostages was disposed of in Chapter 49:

We will immediately restore all hostages and charters (*written promises of fidelity*) delivered to us by Englishmen, as sureties of the peace or of faithful service.

The complaints of Roger de Cressi, Robert de Vaux and many others were satisfied by Chapter 55, for all unjust payments of money as penalties were to be restored. Here the barons showed how much they valued Stephen Langton's counsel, for he was mentioned by name and appointed to judge questions of unjust fines and amercements along with the council of twenty-five:

All fines made with us unjustly and against the law of the land, and all amercements imposed unjustly and against the law of the land, shall be entirely remitted, or else it shall be done concerning them according to the decision of the five-and-twenty barons . . . or according to the judgment of the majority of the same, along with . . . Stephen Langton, Archbishop of Canterbury, if he can be present, and such others as he may wish to bring with him. . . .

Even closer to the archbishop's heart was Chapter 20, which protected all Englishmen from unjust penalties in the future:

A free man shall not be amerced for a slight offense, except in accordance with the degree of his offense; and for a grave offense he shall be amerced in accordance with the gravity of the offense, yet saving always his contenement (*his means of living not to be seized to pay a fine*); and a merchant in the same way, saving his merchandise (*his stock of goods*); and a villein shall be amerced in the same way, saving his wainage (*his horses, oxen, wagons and implements*) if they have fallen upon our mercy; and none of the aforesaid amercements shall be imposed except by the oath (*sworn testimony*) of honest men of the neighborhood.

The lands—and there were many of them, some of vast extent and value—unlawfully seized by the King to avenge himself upon his enemies or to enrich himself were to be restored. Chapter 52 read:

If anyone has been dispossessed or removed by us, without the legal judgment of his peers, from his lands, castles, franchises, or from his right, we will immediately restore them to him; and if a dispute arise over this, then let it be decided by the five-and-twenty barons. . . .

Another section had to do with the King's unlawful seizure of lands for debt to the Crown. He had often sold such property for much more than the amount of the debt, and then kept all the money. Chapter 9 outlined a new system for repaying debts to the Crown which would end such practices.

Nicholas de Stutville, Peter de Bruce, Robert de Vere and all the rest who had either paid the King outrageous sums to obtain their inheritances or had been refused them, were appeased by Chapters 2 and 3:

If any of our earls or barons or others holding of us . . . shall have died, and at the time of his death his heir shall be of full age and owe relief he shall have his inheritance on payment of the ancient relief, namely the heir or heirs of an earl £100 for a whole earl's barony; the heir or heirs of a baron £100 for a whole barony; the heir or heirs of a knight 100 shillings at most for a whole knight's fee (*about five hundred acres of land*); and whoever owes less, let him give less, according to the ancient custom of fiefs.

If, however, the heir of any one of the aforesaid has been under age and in wardship, let him have his inheritance without relief and without fine when he comes of age.

As for John's highhanded sale of guardianships to unscrupulous custodians, Chapter 4 sternly forbade the evil practices by which the property of heirs who were under age had been stripped and ruined, and prescribed penalties for those who disobeyed:

The guardian of the land of an heir who is thus under age, shall take from the land of the heir nothing but reasonable produce, reasonable customs, and reasonable services, and that without destruction or waste of men or goods; and if we have committed the wardship . . . to the sheriff, or to any other who is responsible to us . . . and he has made destruction or waste of what he holds in wardship, we will take of him amends . . . and if we have given or sold the wardship of any such land to anyone and he has therein made destruction or waste, he shall lose that wardship. . . .

An additional section, Chapter 5, provided that guardians must keep up the property while they had custody of it, and return it in good condition when the heir came of age.

An end was made to the King's habit of imposing high scutages and other taxes when he needed money. Chapter 12 provided that except for certain levies which had long been allowed by feudal custom, such taxes should only be collected after approval by a Common Council composed of the archbishops, bishops, abbots, earls and those barons who were large landholders.

Nor was John to be allowed to continue seizing provisions whenever he needed them unless they were paid for in cash. Chapter 28 forbade it, while Chapter 30 kept him from taking horses or carts without the permission of their owners.

No longer was the King to enrich himself by selling widows in marriage. Chapter 8 allowed them to remain unmarried as long as they wished. And Chapter 7 required their inheritances to be given them promptly.

John's tyrannies over his subjects who lived in or near royal forests were to be halted. Twelve knights of each county were to inquire into "all evil customs" connected with the forests and forest officers, and abolish them. And no longer must those living just outside a forest attend the forest courts unless accused of violating forest law or if there were some other good reason for their being present.

The King's foreign favorites were to be removed from their well-paid jobs, and Englishmen who knew the law and would carry it out justly were to be appointed in their places. So outraged were the barons at some of these French interlopers that they added a special chapter listing them by name. As for the mercenary soldiers from France, they were to be banished.

There were a dozen or more other chapters, but since they were of lesser importance to Magna Carta as a great document, they need not be discussed.

On Friday, June 19, the Great Charter was ready. It is a wonder that the royal clerks did not all have writer's cramp, for they had been sweating like cart horses night and day to finish the final draft and then make several copies. They wrote in Latin, the language of scholars and the Church, and with infinite labor reproduced the Charter in a script so neat and fine that it looked almost like printing, each line straight and even, the capital letters in bold black which made them stand out clearly.

Grandly, the preamble began:

John by the grace of God King of England, followed by all his other titles, then listed those in the King's party by name, acknowledging the advice they had given him, and went on to state that the barons' demands were granted.

There followed important Chapter 1, declaring first that the Church of England should be free, then that all free men in the kingdom were to have these rights and liberties forever.

Magna Carta says "all free men." What about the poor villeins who, although they were not actually slaves, were not free? It would have been better if the Great Charter had instead granted its freedoms to "all men." But in effect, very few of its chapters affected villeins, anyhow.

A villein was considered a chattel, a piece of personal property belonging to the landholder whom he served in return for being allowed to gain a living by tilling his master's land. About the only way the King could persecute him was to persecute his master, and Magna Carta forbade this.

True, a villein could be fined unjustly for some misdemeanor, and if he could not pay, his rude plow or other implements could be seized and sold. But that would make it impossible for him to raise his crops, which he had to share with the landholder. The barons had thought of that. Chapter 20 is the only one which mentions villeins, when it says that a villein shall not be unjustly amerced, and that his implements shall not be seized to pay such a fine.

In practically every other way a villein was protected by Magna Carta simply because he was considered the property of his master, and thus injustices he suffered were injustices against his master. It was not a perfect arrangement, but no one has ever called Magna Carta a perfect document. It was only the cornerstone upon which an edifice of freedom for English-speaking people would gradually rise through the years.

And now, at Runnymede, wax had been heated. The clerks applied it to each of the original copies they had prepared, and John affixed his great seal to them.

Outside the tent on the field, the heralds trumpeted a summons. From its encampment, the rebel barons' army assembled and formed ranks, its men and beasts standing motionless as the King, his party and the opposing barons emerged from the tent and took up places on the meadow.

Stephen Langton stepped forward, facing John of England, who placed his hand upon the Bible the archbishop held.

"Do you, John King of England, Lord of Ireland, Duke of Normandy and Aquitaine, and Count of Anjou, swear that the conditions of this charter shall be kept in good faith and without evil intent?"

"We swear it," John promised.

Turning to the rebel barons, Langton administered a similar oath to them. Then they knelt before the King and renewed the oath of fealty and homage they had forsworn, binding them to serve him in war and peace.

The great document known as Magna Carta had come into being and was the law of the land.

Again, with a great flourish, the trumpets blared. There in the meadow, smoke was rising from fires in great pits which had been dug. To the noses of all came savory odors of roasting meat from whole oxen turning slowly on spits, as well as haunches of venison brought by the King's huntsmen from the forest of Windsor. Casks of ale and loaves from the bakehouses of Windsor Castle had been carted to Runnymede, and trestle tables set up to accommodate the dignitaries.

As the meat and drink were served, merriment and good fellowship seemed to prevail among all. The King, still holding his temper in check, played the genial host. For the rest of the day feasting and wassail ruled on the meadow of Runnymede.

It was only after he had returned to Windsor Castle that the King erupted in a frenzy. In his apartments there he raged and blasphemed, cursing his dead mother and the hour she had borne him, gnashing his teeth and trying to crunch an oaken staff into bits. Failing, he took it in his shaking hands and shivered it to flinders like a knight's lance in the shock of combat, while his attendants cowered and dodged lest their heads be broken in the same manner as he flung himself about.

John had no idea that the document to which he had just put his seal would be one of the great foundations of free men's liberties for all time. Neither did the barons who had forced it upon him as they rode off to their captured stronghold of London. Stephen Langton alone had some conception of what it could mean to the people of England, but his heart was heavy with doubt and apprehension for its fate.

Nor did John have the slightest intention of keeping the solemn oath he had sworn to obey Magna Carta. He would do what he might have to in order to make the barons think he was in earnest, but from the start of the negotiations he had been resolved that the Great Charter should be nullified, destroyed and forgotten.

He lost no time in dispatching an envoy to Rome with a demand that Pope Innocent annul Magna Carta.

12

John made a fine show of carrying out his promises, but the rebel barons were suspicious. They kept possession of London, as Magna Carta permitted them to do until their demands had been met. There FitzWalter and the others discussed the King's intentions.

"Marry, 'twould seem he means to obey the charter of liberties," said one. "He promptly sent letters patent to his sheriffs in all the shires, ordering them to carry out its provisions and see that the inhabitants took oath to support our committee of twenty-five."

"Aye," added another, "and he has already removed some of the cursed Frenchmen who have cheated us of posts in his government. That spawn of the Evil One, Engelard de Cigogné, has been forced to give up his sheriff's office, as well as Geoffrey de Martini and Peter de Cancellis theirs as constables of castles. And the worst tyrant of them all, Peter des Roches, has been removed as justiciar."

"But the King has replaced them with his own supporters," a third baron objected. "And while he has freed hostages and sent his French troops at Dover home, we do not know that the rest of the foreign soldiers have left."

"Nor has he restored all of the lands he seized unlawfully," was another complaint. "I say he is uncommonly slow in making good his promises. Let us be cautious."

"You are right," said FitzWalter. "We must remain under arms, and be especially careful that the King has no chance to take London. In respect of that, what of the tournament I am told is being planned to take place at Stamford?"

"It should provide us rare sport, my Lord Robert," said one of the younger knights among his officers. "A lady there has offered to give a bear to him whose skill at the lists prevails over all."

FitzWalter was frowning. "But why is it to be held at a place so distant from London? Intelligence has reached me that a plan is afoot to seize the city."

"Who would dare?" cried a baron.

" 'Certain persons' were the words of the warning," replied the army's commander. "Our absence at Stamford might give the King the very chance he hopes for. Let the tournament instead be held at Hounslow, whence we can ride to the city in a trice upon an alarm of an approaching force. Meanwhile, I pray all of you to be watchful of the King's actions."

They had good cause to be watchful. What John had done to obey the provisions of Magna Carta had been because he dared not do otherwise. But his gesture in sending some of the foreign mercenary soldiers home was a ruse to lull the barons' suspicions. Soon afterward he secretly dispatched officers to Aquitaine and Flanders to recruit more troops. At the same time he saw to it that his chain of strong castles all through the western part of the Midlands were well manned and provisioned.

John would have liked nothing better than to swoop down on London while the rebels were jousting and reveling at Stamford, for the recapture of the metropolis would have strengthened his position immensely. But it was better not to move openly until he had the Pope's reply to his appeal.

Innocent III had not yet received it, but he had the King's earlier complaint of the barons' actions against him, and Stephen Langton's support of them. One day in midsummer, the archbishop called together the suffragan bishops of his see of Canterbury at his archiepiscopal palace. The suffragans saw at once that he was greatly agitated.

"I have received a letter signed by the Bishop of Winchester, the Abbot of Reading and the papal legate, Cardinal Pandulf," Langton began, holding up the parchment for them to see. "The Holy Father in Rome has appointed them to carry out certain commands."

For a moment the archbishop scanned the letter. His voice trembled as he went on: "His Holiness charges that I and some of my bishops are accomplices, if not sharers, in a wicked conspiracy against the King. He has excommunicated the barons, and I am directed to see that the excommunication is published in every church in England. If I fail to do so I am to be suspended from office."

The ranking bishop among the suffragans spoke: "We shall do as you ask, my Lord Archbishop, and publish the excommunication in our churches."

"No!" cried Langton, "I do not ask that you publish it, nor shall I order any clergyman in England to do so. Neither do I order you not to publish it, for I would thus cause you to be suspended, and I do not wish to do that. Each of you must decide for himself."

"But you, my Lord Archbishop!" exclaimed another of the bishops, "if you do not order us to do so you will be disobeying the Holy Father's order, and . . ."

"His Holiness does not understand," the archbishop interposed. "His order is meant only to punish men who are in revolt against the Crown. He has not yet heard that the barons are at peace with the King now that the charter of liberties has been signed. Once the news reaches Rome, the Pope will surely revoke the excommunications."

As he spoke he saw more than one among them shake his head in disbelief. He dismissed them then, and they left him, stunned and disheartened, to meditate upon what had happened. His old friend in Rome had deserted him. Innocent III, one of the ablest and most learned popes of his time, had been misled by John's submission to the Church. And with the caustic words of the pontiff's letter still burning in his ears, the archbishop realized that the barons' excommunication would mean civil war, and that Magna Carta was doomed.

A few weeks later, Stephen Langton summoned his suffragans to Canterbury once more. He was pale and shaken as he faced them.

"I have called you here to bid you farewell," he said. "Those whom the Pope appointed his agents to carry out his commands have informed me that because of my failure to cooperate in publishing the excommunication of the barons, I have been suspended from office."

"What will you do, my Lord Archbishop?" cried one of the bishops.

"I shall resign my seat of Canterbury and go to France.

The Carthusian monks there devote their lives to contemplation, prayer, study and labor. I shall become one of them."

Another suffragan rose, holding up his hands in protest. "But the Carthusian monastery of La Grande Chartreuse is in an Alpine wilderness, my Lord Archbishop! For a man of your wisdom and abilities to be cloistered there, isolated from the world! . . ."

Langton bowed his head. "I have failed to achieve the great purpose of my life. It is better that I spend the rest of it in humble submission to the will of God, and in penance for my sins."

"But you have met failure before—and vanquished it! You will do so again, my Lord Archbishop! In the name of God and Holy Church, I beg you, reconsider!"

For some moments Stephen Langton sat slumped in his chair, his eyes closed. Suddenly he opened them and sat erect.

"You are right," he said. "I have not yet lost my struggle for men's liberties! I will go to Rome, plead with the Holy Father and make him see the truth. Surely he will listen to reason. . . ."

The archbishop packed a few belongings and set out like a pilgrim on his long journey. But even as he fared south, a second letter from the Pope was on its way north.

The King, Innocent had written, had been forced to make a vile, wicked, illegal and iniquitous agreement which had degraded his rights and his honor.

"The charter," concluded the letter, "with all understandings and guarantees, whether conforming to or resulting from it, we declare to be null and void of all validity forever."

Indeed, it did seem that Magna Carta was dead, and doomed to be forgotten. By the time the Pope's letter reached

England, the barons' suspicions of the King's movements had stirred them to action, and civil war was already raging.

From London, Robert FitzWalter led a force of his soldiers eastward toward Dover, where John was awaiting the arrival of his new host of foreign troops. Blocking the rebels' way over the Dover Road stood the King's great stronghold of Rochester Castle.

It was commanded by Reginald de Cornhill, whose family had long stood high in the royal favor. But Cornhill allied himself with the rebels and opened the castle gates to them.

The infuriated King marched from Dover and laid siege to the castle.

"Smash down the walls!" he commanded with a curse. "As soon as a breach is opened in them we will storm the place!"

Mighty catapults were moved into position. For seven weeks they hurled massive boulders and millstones at the castle, but its walls were so thick and strong that the missiles bounded off harmlessly.

Meanwhile, another plan, suggested by a resourceful officer and eagerly seized upon by the frustrated King, was being carried out. Soldiers laboriously dug a tunnel under the castle walls and shored it with timbers.

"Get me a herd of pigs," this officer said when the tunnel was ready.

A detachment of soldiers rounded up the animals as they foraged in the countryside.

"Tie flaming torches to them and let them loose in the tunnel," was the next order.

In their frantic rush, the pigs set fire to the timbers, the tunnel collapsed, and with it a corner of the castle's keep. John's men charged in, took the stronghold and held the

rebel commander, William d'Albini, and his officers for
ransom.

The King's strength had increased considerably since the
day of Runnymede. Some of the foreign troops had arrived
and joined him at Rochester. Out of a little more than two
hundred castles in England, he and his supporters held about
one hundred and fifty. And he had a source of revenue the
rebels did not enjoy, for the profitable tin mines of Devon
and Cornwall were in royal hands.

The rebels countered this strength by inviting Philip
Augustus of France to join them, offering the crown of England to his son Louis if he would help them. Although Philip
was not enthusiastic, Louis was, and the French king finally
agreed to let him lead an army to England.

John massed his navy at the mouth of the Thames to repel
the invasion, and moved toward the sea to be ready in case
the French succeeded in landing. Soon afterward a terrible
storm lashed the Channel coast. At his headquarters, the
King received disquieting news.

"Many of our ships are wrecked and the rest scattered,"
he was told. "Louis and his army are crossing the Channel."

The King decided not to risk a decisive battle with Louis'
army. If he lost, and his force were wiped out, he would lose
everything. Also since he owed his French mercenary soldiers
their pay, he was afraid they might desert to their country-
men. He left a strong English garrison at Dover Castle and
retired westward.

The French landed and marched to London, taking the
castles of Canterbury and Rochester on the way. A few weeks
later, John received more bad news.

"The French have taken the two castles at Winchester,
Sire," William Marshal reported to him. "The news has

caused a number of our supporters to join the rebels. Your kinsman Salisbury is among them, I regret to say, as well as the Earls of Arundel and Warren and the Count of Aumale."

Hearing this, some of John's officers were certain the royal cause was lost, since the deserters controlled thirteen important castles and the services of many knights.

"What of our castle at Dover?" John demanded.

"The French have been unable to take it, my liege," replied Marshal.

"Then they do not control the southwestern counties. We are not beaten, nor shall we be. The rest of our castles still stand fast against this traitorous enemy. As for the rebels' castles, we have taken or destroyed many, and their lands have been ravaged."

"Aye," Marshal agreed, "and there are reports that their leaders are at odds with the French barons who came with Louis, and whom they rightly suspect of casting a greedy eye upon English lands."

"We shall continue to fight until this rebellion is crushed and the rebels destroyed," the King decreed.

Fight they did, all up and down England, though at no time was the full strength of the opposing armies massed against each other. The summer passed, and it was now September, 1216. The civil war had been in progress for a year, and Magna Carta, with its solemn provisions for law and order, might as well have been torn to bits and the pieces flung to the winds.

Then Fate took a hand. The royal army, sweeping through Norfolk, reached the town of Lynn, which welcomed the King and feasted him—feasted him too well in an age when sanitation and refrigeration of food were unknown, for he fell ill of dysentery.

Nevertheless, they moved on into Lincolnshire. At low tide, while the troops were crossing a part of the wide estuary called The Wash, the tide turned swiftly. All the army's carts, wagons, their horses and John's treasury, with its store of coin and a fabulous trove of gold and silver goblets, flagons, ornaments and coronation regalia, including the royal crown, were lost in the quicksands as the flood swept in. The King himself barely escaped.

Sick in both body and soul, John went on to the Bishop of Lincoln's castle of Newark, where he was put to bed with a raging fever. The Abbot of Croxton, famed for his medical skill, was summoned, but he could do nothing. On October 18, 1216, John, King of England, died.

A strange, almost miraculous thing then happened. Little Prince Henry, heir to the throne, had been placed for safekeeping in one of the King's strongholds in the Midlands. With his mother, Queen Isabella, he was hurriedly taken to Gloucester Castle. Although the great crown was lost, the Queen produced a golden circlet, and with it the loyalist barons crowned nine-year-old Henry III, and made William Marshal regent to rule until the boy king should come of age.

Then, a few days later, the loyal barons held a solemn meeting at Bristol. In the name of Henry III they reissued the Great Charter, and declared all its provisions in full effect.

Magna Carta was not dead. It had been resurrected, not by the rebel barons who had wrung it from King John, but by his own supporters.

13

No, Magna Carta was not dead. It lived, and it would continue to live, its power for orderly government and the rights of man becoming ever stronger.

All Stephen Langton's pleadings with Innocent III failed to change the pontiff's mind about the charter, but he allowed his old friend to remain in Rome during his suspension. There, while the civil war was still raging in England during the summer of 1216, Innocent died. A good and gentle man, Honorius III, whose reign was one of peacemaking in a Europe torn by wars, ascended to the papal throne.

When the loyalist barons reissued Magna Carta, it was not annulled by Rome, nor was it in 1217, when it was revised and reconfirmed, with its provisions relating to the forests put into a separate document called the Charter of the Forest.

For a time the rebel barons and their French ally, Prince Louis, continued the war, but after an armada bringing reinforcements from France was almost destroyed by the English navy, peace was restored, and the rebels swore allegiance to Henry III.

As regent, William Marshal ruled wisely and well. The barons found little cause to complain that Magna Carta was not being observed. When Marshal died in 1219, the same was true of his successor, Hubert de Burgh.

Meanwhile, Pope Honorius had lifted Stephen Langton's suspension, and he returned to England, Archbishop of Canterbury once more. Although he had had nothing to do with the resurrection of Magna Carta, he was content to see the English people's guarantee of liberties restored. However, he was yet to achieve a final triumph which would give him the satisfaction of having had a vital part in Magna Carta's firm establishment.

The young King was growing up. Fearing that he might bring back his father's evil customs once he took over the rule of England, the barons felt he should reissue Magna Carta under his own hand and seal. They discussed it with Stephen Langton and asked him to speak for them before the King.

The conference was held in January, 1224, at Westminster in the presence of Henry and his court.

"May it please you, Sire," Stephen Langton began, "it is not possible for you to avoid granting this petition of your barons. At the time peace was restored, and the French prince departed from the kingdom, both you and the barons who had been in rebellion against your father took oath to observe the charter of liberties granted by the late King. Thus for you to refuse to confirm it would violate your oath."

Not all of Henry's counselors favored continuing Magna Carta. Without it, not only the King's power but their own would be much greater. One of them, William Brewer, spoke out belligerently: "The liberties which you demand, my Lord Archbishop, having been extorted by force from the late King John, ought not to be observed."

Angered by Brewer's arrogance, Langton rebuked him: "William, if you loved the King you would not thus stand in the way of the peace of the kingdom."

At sixteen, young King Henry already had a mind of his own, and now he spoke it: "We have sworn to observe all these liberties, and what we have sworn to, we are bound to abide by."

In spite of the King's declaration, those of his counselors who were against Magna Carta managed to block his confirmation of it for over a year. At last, however, to raise needed revenues, the regent and the counselors proposed to levy a heavy tax upon all chattels, or movable property.

The barons seized their chance. "Under the charter of liberties," they pointed out, "such a tax may not be imposed except by the consent of the Common Council of archbishops, bishops, abbots, earls and high-ranking barons. Unless the King reissues the charter we will block the tax."

The royal counselors yielded. Magna Carta had won its first important victory. And now Stephen Langton had his triumph at an impressive ceremony held on February 11, 1225, in Westminster Hall. The gallery which encircled its interior was jammed with spectators that day, while the benches on the floor below were filled with nobility and high-ranking clergy. The seventeen-year-old King was there, seated on an elevated throne. About him were his Council, Stephen Langton, and high dignitaries of the Church.

Then a procession of priests and monks entered the hall with slow, measured tread. Each carried a candle, and as they came in, the dimness of the hall was transformed into a golden glow. When they had halted before the dais, clerks applied hot wax to copies of the reissued Great Charter and its companion Charter of the Forest, and King Henry affixed his great seal to them, while Stephen Langton, eleven of his bishops, twenty abbots, nine earls and twenty-three barons attested to it as witnesses.

Then Langton, reading from a book, pronounced the sentence of excommunication upon anyone who henceforth should violate Magna Carta. When he had concluded, the priests and monks threw their candles to the floor, extinguishing them, and in the background a bell was tolled in the ancient rite of excommunication by bell, book and candle.

Now, having prevented Magna Carta from being extinguished, the archbishop could feel that he had fulfilled the great aspiration of his life. He knew he hadn't many years left, but he could spend them in the peace of mind that comes from accomplishment.

It has always been true that, once any freedom has been gained, it must be preserved against those who would take it away. Magna Carta was no exception. Many times in the next four centuries it was in danger of sinking into oblivion, yet always it was kept alive by those who enjoyed its liberties.

Under Henry III, Magna Carta was often threatened. His character was very different from that of his father. He had high principles, was devoted to the Church, had charming manners and was interested in art and literature. But for all these praiseworthy traits, Henry was constantly in trouble with the barons because of unwise projects which required a great deal of money, and the ways he took to raise it.

For a time, whenever the King proposed a new tax to finance one of his schemes, the barons agreed. Meanwhile, however, in his efforts to raise revenues from every possible source, Henry had allowed his sheriffs, bailiffs, forest wardens and other royal officers to slip back into their old ways of oppression. Against the provisions of Magna Carta, unjust fines were being collected in the courts, and justice sold. Once again the royal privilege of purveyance was being abused.

In 1237, when the King asked for another tax, the barons resisted. "Confirm Magna Carta again, and swear to observe it," they told him, "or we will not allow you to raise the money you need."

They said this not once, but five times during his long reign of fifty-six years. Henry always obeyed promptly. In fact, he was so charming and gracious about it that the barons felt a little contrite at having been so insistent. But after each confirmation the King gradually lapsed into his former practices.

It was much the same with his son, who came to the throne in 1272 as Edward I. Twice in his thirty-five-year reign, the barons demanded and got a reconfirmation of Magna Carta.

During this time, something tremendously important to the future of England's government, and later to that of the United States, was taking place. Chapter 61 of Magna Carta, setting up the committee of twenty-five barons to enforce it, was one of its all-important provisions because it established that the King was not above the law.

After Magna Carta came into being at Runnymede, Chapter 61 was never again included when the charter was reissued, yet the right of a group of English subjects to control the King's actions had been recognized. And control was still exercised by the Common Council of prelates, earls and ranking barons.

One of the chief historians and writers who lived during this period, Matthew Paris, began to call the Council a parliament about the year 1246. And when it met in 1255 to demand a new confirmation of Magna Carta, the official records referred to it as a parliament.

As the years passed, other changes were made in the composition of this group of subjects who kept the King from violating the law. Gradually, from the beginning which was Chapter 61 of Magna Carta, the English Parliament, with its House of Commons, elected by the people, came into existence to enact the laws of England.

In the century which passed after Edward I's reign, Magna Carta was continually threatened by the kings who followed him. Between 1307 and 1422, it was reconfirmed thirty-seven times. In the tumultuous reign of Edward II there were seventeen of these affirmations.

Then the House of Tudor came to the English throne. During this period, especially under the powerful rule of Henry VIII and his daughter, the famous Queen Elizabeth I, Parliament was so subjugated to the royal will that one historian said Magna Carta "rested in the shade."

Yet while the Tudors ruled, the Great Charter's strength increased immensely. No longer did scholarly monks labor for weeks and months to turn out a single parchment manuscript, beautifully illuminated, but which could be read by only a few. The printing press had been introduced into England. Now that their manuscripts could be read by many, people were writing as they never had before. Some took Magna Carta for their subject, and the outstanding among these was Sir Edward Coke.

Coke was one of the greatest lawyers England has ever seen. Malefactors trembled when this aristocratic and imposing figure, with a long face made even longer by a pointed beard, prosecuted them as a Crown attorney. Once he put his nose like a hound's to the scent, he relentlessly pursued his quarry to the kill in collecting evidence and presenting it clearly and forcefully in court. As attorney-general he prosecuted Sir Walter Raleigh for treason and secured his conviction, for which Raleigh was eventually beheaded. When plotters tried to blow up the Houses of Parliament in 1604—the Gunpowder Plot which is celebrated today with fireworks in England—Coke's brilliant prosecution sent Guy Fawkes and others of the conspirators to the gallows.

But Sir Edward's greatest accomplishments were his writings on the law. He knew Magna Carta from beginning to end, and considered it the greatest of all documents in English law. In 1629 he published the second of his *Institutes,* a classic of legal knowledge in which he interpreted the chapters of Magna Carta, showing their meaning in English law and their effect upon it.

Coke knew the importance of Chapter 39 of Magna Carta, forbidding the King to seize a man or his lands and to imprison, outlaw or otherwise persecute him without due process of law. In quaint and occasionally misspelled language, he wrote about it:

As the goldfiner will not out of the dust, threds or shreds of Gold, let pass the least crum, in respect to the excellency of the metal; so ought not the learned Reader to let pass any syllable of this law, in respect of the excellency of the matter.

Coke made good use of Magna Carta in defending innocent persons. Most often, King James I was his target.

James had no use for Magna Carta. He believed in the divine right of kings, the doctrine which says that since a monarch's right to rule comes directly from God, he can do no wrong. Sir Edward devoted a great deal of his time to showing James how wrong he was. The King retaliated by having him arrested for urging Parliament not to be submissive to the ruler, and for a time Coke was shut up in the Tower of London.

The King had his favorites, upon whom he lavished favors. To one he granted a monopoly for making gold and silver thread, used in the gorgeous costumes of that period. The other goldsmiths were outraged. When their protests were ignored, they went ahead and made the thread anyway. James had some arrested and thrown into prison; the shops of others were broken into, and their tools seized. Then the King tried to make them put up bonds to insure they would not infringe on the monopoly, threatening that if they refused he would fill all the prisons in London with violators and leave them there to rot.

London was in such an uproar that Parliament took a hand. Coke was then a member of the House of Commons. He made a speech charging the King had violated Chapter 39 of Magna Carta. The lawmakers agreed, and James was forced to release the prisoners and end the monopoly.

Charles I, almost as arbitrary as James, also found Coke a formidable opponent who was always blocking his plans. He appointed Sir Edward sheriff of Buckinghamshire to get rid of him, but soon afterward Coke got himself elected to Parliament from that county, and was right back defending Magna Carta and the rest of English law against the King.

Coke was so fond of quoting Magna Carta in the courts and in Parliament that his colleagues made jokes about it. And while by his use of the Great Charter he often turned the joke against them, once they had the last laugh.

The Lord Treasurer of England had been accused of misconduct in office and was brought to trial before the court of the Star Chamber in Westminster Hall. Coke prosecuted the case for the Crown.

The Lord Treasurer was convicted. Sir Edward then pleaded that the cabinet officer should be severely punished.

"In view of the seriousness of my Lord Treasurer's offense in an office of public trust, I suggest a fine of one hundred thousand pounds," he told the august judges.

The chief attorney for the defense leaped to his feet. "I protest, your Lordships, that such a fine is excessive and in violation of *salvo contenemento!*" Then, as the rest of the lawyers in the court grinned, he began quoting Chapter 20 of Magna Carta:

" 'A free man shall not be amerced for a slight offense, except in accordance with the degree of his offense; and for a grave offense he shall be amerced in accordance with the gravity of the offense, yet saving always his contenement. . . . ' "

And he went on: "*Salvo contenemento,* as your Lordships know, stems from this chapter of Magna Carta, meaning that no man shall be fined so much that his means of livelihood are taken away. I submit that a fine of one hundred thousand pounds would so impoverish my Lord Treasurer that he could not continue to exist."

The judges agreed with him, and the fine was reduced to thirty thousand pounds. And since Sir Edward was the last man in England to object when Magna Carta was called upon to defend an English subject, he probably enjoyed the joke as much as his fellow lawyers.

As time went on, Charles I became more and more tyrannical. At last Parliament resolved to force him to observe the

rights and liberties of English subjects. The King's answer
to their demand was that Magna Carta and other laws concerning freedoms were still in force, and he would maintain
them. It made no difference whether his promise was in writing, he said. His royal word was all they needed.

The members of the Parliament were not so trustful of
the royal word. They put their demands into writing in a
petition and demanded that Charles sign it. Coke was one
of those who drafted the document, and of course he referred
to Magna Carta a number of times. The King finally yielded,
and signed what is known as the Petition of Right.

Another great bulwark of English liberties had come into
being. A number of its provisions had developed straight out
of Magna Carta. One was that no man should be imprisoned
without cause.

Because of that provision, the Petition of Right has been
called the first Habeas Corpus Act. *Habeas corpus* is a Latin
phrase meaning "produce the body." When a man is arrested for wrongdoing and confined, his lawyer may obtain
a writ of *habeas corpus*. It is an order that the accused man
be brought into court (his body produced), and released on
bail unless the judge decides his crime is so serious that he
must be held in prison. In any case he must be tried as soon
as possible if he demands it.

Some writers have claimed that *habeas corpus* originated
with Magna Carta's famous Chapter 39. It did not, for the
right of a man not to be held in prison without cause goes
far back beyond the Great Charter. Chapter 39 merely confirmed that ancient right. The Petition of Right confirmed it
again; some years later the actual Habeas Corpus Act established it firmly, with provisions for its enforcement. But
Coke and the others who wrote the Petition of Right went

to Chapter 39 of Magna Carta for this clause, which in time developed into the Habeas Corpus Act.

Charles learned no lesson from the Petition of Right and continued his oppressions until, in 1649, having been convicted of high treason, he was beheaded, the first and last of the English kings to be executed. He himself was protected by Magna Carta, for it was only after a trial conducted under its safeguards for accused persons that he was sentenced to death. And in this terrible manner the principle which is the very heart and soul of the Great Charter was sustained: The King is not above the law.

Then came Oliver Cromwell, the stern Puritan who ruled England as Protector after Charles I's son was forced to flee from the kingdom. Cromwell, the dictator, had only contempt for Magna Carta, and scoffed when it was invoked against his actions. Yet after his death, when Charles II came to the throne in the Restoration, the Great Charter resumed its power to guarantee the freedoms of English subjects.

Never again was it seriously threatened. Many of its provisions, of course, ceased to have meaning with the end of feudalism in England. But it remains today a mighty foundation of the British Constitution which, unlike that of the United States, is not a written document, but simply all the great principles which underlie British law.

Meanwhile, the power of Magna Carta for orderly government and freedom was spreading across the sea. Settlement in the New World had begun.

In England's American colonies, the leaders took the view that they had inherited all the rights of Englishmen. Thanks to Sir Edward Coke and other writers on English law, these earliest of American statesmen knew Magna Carta and considered it a bulwark of their rights.

In almost every one of the colonies, as the leaders established the laws under which their governments operated, they
turned to Magna Carta.

14

In 1630 a band of Puritans from England came to America and founded Boston. They had a charter granted by Charles I for the settlement of the Massachusetts Bay Colony. In it, strangely enough, this King who believed in allowing no one to have ruling power except himself, permitted the colonists to govern themselves, provided they enacted no laws which violated those of England. He seems to have given very little thought to it, looking on the colony merely as a trading post which might thus bring revenues into his treasury. And he was always glad to be rid of his Puritan enemies, who sought in Parliament to curb his power.

Under their charter, the settlers elected a governor, a deputy governor and a council of eighteen called assistants, though they became better known as magistrates. These twenty men formed the General Court, passed the laws and governed the colony.

For five years the General Court ran the colony about as it pleased. It was almost as bad a form of government as that in which King John had wielded his wicked power over England. The laws which the General Court passed were never printed, but lay buried under piles of other handwritten records. Persons accused of crimes and those who brought suits over land ownership and other disputes were not allowed to see the records; neither were their lawyers.

If there was no law to cover a case brought before the magistrates, who also sat as judges, they used their own ideas in deciding it. Men were fined or severely punished for offenses which were not even included in the far more extensive laws of England. Some were banished from the colony when no offense had been charged; the magistrates simply noted that such persons were "not fit to live with us."

In 1635 Governor John Winthrop made a proposal that did not please the magistrates at all. During a session of the General Court, he said, "The people think their condition very unsafe while so much power rests in the direction of the magistrates. Some men should be appointed to frame a body of principles of laws in resemblance to a Magna Carta, which should be received for fundamental laws."

These were austere men who sat before him in their dark homespun, its somberness relieved only by the square white collars or great ruffs at their necks.

"Why should we have a body of laws?" one of them demanded. "We have no trouble in governing the colony. The only law we need is the Word of God."

Like the kings of England, the magistrates were alarmed at anything which threatened their power. Nevertheless, they appointed a committee to study the subject and draw up a code of laws. It accomplished little, however. But in 1641,

Richard Bellingham, who had succeeded Winthrop as governor, brought the subject up again.

"The people are restless," he told the magistrates. "It is time something was done to enact a code of laws. Nathaniel Ward is not only a brilliant preacher, but studied and practiced law in England before he entered the ministry. I will ask him to draw up such a code."

But when Mr. Ward's document was submitted, more than one of the magistrates frowned and shook his head after reading it.

One raised his hands in abhorrence. "This body of laws smacks of heresy!" he declared. "Mr. Ward does not seem to have relied entirely upon the Scriptures in preparing it."

"True," said another, "yet it sets forth clearly the rights of our people as Englishmen. Let us call Mr. Ward in and question him about the sources he has used."

Ward was summoned before the General Court. "You asked me to draw up a code of laws," he told the magistrates. "I am sure you are familiar with the renown of the late Sir Edward Coke. . . ."

Most of the men nodded, among them John Winthrop, who was now one of the magistrates, and who had studied law at Cambridge University in England.

"Sir Edward led the Puritan party in Parliament in opposition to that of the king," Ward went on. "He had a leading part in drafting the Petition of Right which King Charles was forced to grant. In writing it, Coke had recourse to Magna Carta. Since both are great documents, I naturally considered both in drafting this code of laws."

A battle developed over his code, with some of the stiff-necked Puritans opposing it bitterly, but at last they approved a document called the Body of Liberties. It consisted of one hundred fundamental laws upon which government of the Massachusetts Bay colony was to be based.

Some of the provisions of the Body of Liberties were adopted from the Law of Moses and other Scriptural precepts. But others were closely modeled after those of the Petition of Right and Magna Carta. In its very first clause, the principles of four chapters of the Great Charter were embodied: Chapter 39, forbidding the king to seize, imprison or otherwise persecute any free man without due process of law; Chapter 49, concerning hostages; and Chapters 9 and 52, relating to the seizure of land.

This first clause read:

No man's life shall be taken away; no man's honor or good name shall be stained; no man's person shall be arrested, restrained, banished, dismembered, nor anyways punished (*this was like Chapter 39*); no man shall be deprived of his wife or children (*similar to Chapter 49*); no man's goods or estate shall be taken away, nor in any way endangered under color of law, or countenance of authority (*like Chapters 9 and 52*); unless it be by virtue or equity of some express law of the country warranting the same. . . .

Section 8 of the Body of Liberties was similar to Chapters 28 and 30 of Magna Carta concerning purveyance. It forbade the government to seize any man's cattle or goods except as prescribed by law, and then they must be paid for at reasonable rates.

Section 10 was like Chapter 2, in which heirs were allowed to inherit estates without paying exorbitant fines; in the Body of Liberties no one was to pay such a charge at all. Other provisions, not actually in Magna Carta, were modeled upon English law which had developed from the Great Charter, such as the right to trial by jury, and *habeas corpus.*

The Body of Liberties marked the first time an American colony had asserted that the people were entitled to the rights and liberties of Englishmen, but from then on, in all the colonies, the people strove to protect those rights. At last, in 1775, when they believed they had been denied them, they rose in rebellion against England.

It was also the first time an American colony had established a charter of liberties in which the principles of Magna Carta were repeated. But as time went on, most of the colonies either adopted charters embodying the principles of Magna Carta or included clauses stating that the Great Charter was in force there.

Magna Carta was kept much in the minds of the American colonists. In 1687 William Penn, who had founded the colony of Pennsylvania, had the Great Charter printed for the first time in America.

Penn, a great defender of liberty, knew Magna Carta well through his study of law in London as a young man. Persecuted in England because he was a Quaker, he was arrested, imprisoned in the Tower and tried for holding meetings of the Quakers. Penn claimed that Magna Carta guaranteed religious freedom. He quoted the Great Charter so eloquently in his defense that he was found not guilty. When the infuriated judge tried to persuade the jury to change its verdict, it refused.

When Penn drafted a "Frame of Government" for the Pennsylvania colony he included a section providing that Magna Carta and all the English laws which had confirmed it should be in full force as a part of the government of the province. When he published the Great Charter he wrote an introduction saying he had ventured to have it printed because he knew the country had few lawbooks, and he hoped it would be of service to the people by making them resolve not to give up any part of the liberty they enjoyed.

Among the most determined of all colonial settlers to preserve their liberties were those of Massachusetts. On a sultry summer afternoon in 1743, the air of the Cambridge meetinghouse was stifling, and the dignitaries attending the commencement exercises of Harvard College were half dozing after a big dinner as candidates for the degree of master of arts droned out their orations. But suddenly Governor William Shirley and the rest sat bolt upright when the subject of another oration was announced:

"Whether it be lawful to resist the Supreme Magistrate if the Commonwealth cannot otherwise be preserved. An affirmative view of the question by Samuel Adams."

The bigwigs were appalled. It was the first time anyone had asserted publicly in America that rebellion against the king could be justified. This suggested treason.

Probably young Sam Adams, who was to become one of the greatest of the American Revolutionary patriots, had never heard of Stephen Langton. Yet in effect he was defending the same principle that Langton had given his students at the Sorbonne more than five centuries earlier:

"The subject owes obedience only as long as the king acts according to law, and upon the advice of his proper counselors."

Sam Adams undoubtedly did know about Magna Carta, however, although he never studied law. James Otis knew, and Otis was at Harvard with Sam, and his close friend and associate in the years while the Revolution was brewing. Many patriot leaders were thoroughly familiar with it—John

Adams, who as a law clerk had been ordered to toil through Coke's *Institutes* and write a condensed version of them; Thomas Jefferson, who had also mastered the *Institutes*, and said they were "uncouth but cunning learning"; and others.

In 1776, when Adams, Jefferson, Benjamin Franklin, Roger Sherman of Connecticut and Robert Livingston of New York were appointed by the Second Continental Congress to prepare a Declaration of Independence, the great principle of Magna Carta that the king is not above the law was clearly fixed in their minds. One has only to read the Declaration to find phrases which prove it:

> We hold these truths to be self-evident, that all men are created equal, that they are endowed by their Creator with certain unalienable Rights. . . .
>
> . . . That whenever any Form of Government becomes destructive of these ends it is the Right of the People to alter or abolish it. . . .
>
> But when a long train of abuses and usurpations, pursuing invariably the same object, evinces a design to reduce them under absolute Despotism, it is their right, it is their duty, to throw off such Government. . . .

More than five hundred years had passed since King John's barons had altered his form of government by setting up a committee of twenty-five to control his actions. Jefferson and the others who aided him in framing the Declaration of Independence also believed that the then king (George III) had put himself above the law in tyrannical acts toward the American colonies. They, too, were altering their government.

Magna Carta assumed even greater importance when the Constitution of the United States was framed in 1786. Like the Great Charter, and like the Body of Liberties, this was to be a foundation upon which the laws of the new nation would be based. Most important of all its provisions would be those guaranteeing forever the rights and liberties of American citizens.

This was so important that after the Constitution had been ratified by the states, there were many who felt that these rights had not been fully expressed in the Constitution, and that the document must be amended so that there could be no question of what these rights were.

In 1789 James Madison, who had helped to draft the Constitution and was then a member of Congress, drew up ten amendments. These together with several articles of the Constitution itself, are known as the Bill of Rights. Thus, within our Constitution, we have an American Magna Carta which guarantees the precious rights of every American citizen.

Those who framed the Constitution depended greatly upon English law, even though our system of government is different in many respects from that of England. So it is not surprising that a number of the articles of the Bill of Rights came to us, directly or indirectly, from Magna Carta.

Like Chapter 1 of Magna Carta, which states that the English church shall be free, the First Amendment to the Constitution says that Congress shall make no law respecting an establishment of religion, or prohibiting its free exercise.

Famous Chapter 39 of Magna Carta protected all free men from arrest, imprisonment, seizure of their property or other persecution except by due process of law. Our equally famous

Fifth Amendment says in part that no one, except under special circumstances when the country is in danger, shall be deprived of life, liberty or property without due process of law. And like Chapters 28 and 30 of the Great Charter, limiting the king's privilege of purveyance, the Fifth Amendment also states that private property shall not be taken for public use without just compensation.

Some historians have claimed that Chapter 39 of Magna Carta established the right of trial by jury. Actually it did not, because today's form of trial by a jury of twelve persons who must reach a unanimous verdict did not come into use for more than a century after Magna Carta. However, Chapter 39, which used the words "except by lawful judgment of his peers," developed in time into our system of jury trials. Both Article III, Section 2 of the Constitution itself and the Sixth Amendment require trial by jury in criminal cases, while the Seventh Amendment also requires it for all but trivial damage suits.

Chapters 20 and 55 of Magna Carta forbade unjust fines and amercements. The Eighth Amendment to the Constitution says, "Excessive bail shall not be required, nor excessive fines imposed."

Habeas corpus, which grew out of Chapter 39 of Magna Carta, is guaranteed by Article I, Section 9 of the Constitution.

In Chapter 32 of the Great Charter, the King agreed not to hold lands seized from convicted felons for more than a year and a day. Article I, Section 9 of the Constitution forbids Congress to pass any bill of attainder—a bill allowing seizure of property belonging to persons convicted of felony.

Since the Bill of Rights binds only the national government, all the states have adopted similar bills or declarations of rights so that people are protected against injustice or persecution at the hands of any state government.

Thus, in America, those liberties and freedoms of Magna Carta which are still of importance to free men of the twentieth century have been preserved.

Today, in countries where men are not free, people can be—and are—seized and imprisoned without trial, or by a trial in which they have no chance of obtaining true justice. They own no property, for all of it belongs to the government, which holds dictatorial power. While churches may be permitted in these countries, they, too, are not free; their clergy may be imprisoned if they preach what the government does not like to hear. The people have no control over their leaders, but must always do as they are told, and they are allowed to choose these leaders only in elections in which the name of only one candidate for any office is on the ballot, and whom they have had no voice in selecting.

We are free. We cannot be sentenced to imprisonment or any other punishment for a crime unless our guilt is proved beyond reasonable doubt in the minds of a judge or twelve jurors who must all agree on their verdict. We may call as many witnesses as we like to testify for us. And before we are tried we may be released on bail unless there is clear evidence that we may be guilty of a very serious crime. We may own land and other property, and it cannot be taken from us by the government except for a good reason, and we must then be paid a reasonable price for it.

No matter what our religious beliefs, we can worship freely and as we please. We may criticize our leaders and our government as long as we do not urge the overthrow of government by violent means. If a majority of the people do not like the way they are governed they can turn the leaders out by voting against them in an election. The leaders' actions, from the President of the United States down, are also controlled by our representatives in legislative bodies, and by the justices who administer the law in our courts.

All these things had their beginnings in a green meadow beside a placid river on that long-past day of June 15, 1215. How astonished those barons—some greedy, some power-hungry—would be if they could know that what they started in order to gain their own ends had become such a powerful force for right and freedom! For the Great Charter marches on today. As long as men are ready to strive, fight, give their lives for freedom, the great principles of Magna Carta will continue to guard and preserve it.

SUGGESTED FURTHER READING

The list of references consulted in writing this book is very long. Here are a few of the outstanding ones which young students may wish to consult to obtain more detailed knowledge of Magna Carta and its period.

ON MAGNA CARTA

McKechnie, William Sharp. *Magna Carta.* Glasgow: James Maclehose & Sons, 1914. McKechnie is the classic authority on Magna Carta. Contains the Great Charter itself, and the author's comments and interpretation of each chapter's importance and influence on history. Other good commentaries on Magna Carta are contained in the biographies of King John listed below.

ON MAGNA CARTA'S LATER INFLUENCE

Guthrie, William D. "Magna Carta," in *Bench and Bar,* Vol. 10, November, 1915. Magna Carta's influence upon constitutional law in the United States.

Hazeltine, H. D. "The Influence of Magna Carta on Constitutional Development," in *Columbia Law Review,* Vol. 17, January, 1917. How the Great Charter's principles were adopted into our laws and Federal and State constitutions.

Thompson, Faith. *Magna Carta: Its Role in the Making of the English Constitution.* Minneapolis: University of Minnesota Press, 1948. A very detailed study of how the Great Charter affected English law and liberties.

ON KING JOHN

Appleby, John T. *John, King of England.* New York: Alfred A. Knopf, 1959. Well written and easy to read.

Painter, Sidney. *The Reign of King John.* Baltimore: Johns Hopkins Press, 1949. A detailed, scholarly and authoritative reference work by an outstanding American authority.

Warren, W. L. *King John.* London: Eyre & Spottiswoode, 1961. Well written, complete and accurate.

ON MEDIEVAL ENGLAND

Ashley, Maurice. *Great Britain to 1688.* Ann Arbor: University of Michigan Press, 1961. An excellent modern reference work.

Keen, Maurice. *The Outlaws of Medieval England.* London: Routledge & Kegan Paul, 1961. A study of English outlaws of medieval times, including the fantastic adventures of Fulk FitzWarin.

Quennell, M. and C. H. B. *A History of Everyday Things in England.* London: B. T. Batsford, Ltd., 1950. A series of four volumes covering the years 1066 to 1914. Interesting, informative, easy to read and very well illustrated.

Stenton, Doris Mary. "English Society in the Early Middle Ages," in *The Pelican History of England,* Vol. 3. Harmondsworth, Middlesex: Penguin Books, 1952. Interesting, complete and readable, by an authority on England of the Middle Ages.

ON THE WRITS OF ASSISTANCE

Bowen, Catherine Drinker. *John Adams and the American Revolution*. Boston: Little, Brown & Co., 1950. This splendid book on John Adams contains a chapter with a graphic description of James Otis' appearance at the trial in the Writs of Assistance case.

INDEX

185

ABOUT THE AUTHOR

CLIFFORD LINDSEY ALDERMAN was born in Springfield, Massachusetts, educated in public schools there and at the U. S. Naval Academy. He has traveled all over the world, both as a tourist and in connection with his writing, since he likes to know at first hand the places he writes about. He is the author of a number of books, for both adults and young people.